The Graphic Designer's Basic Guide to the Macintosh®

BY MICHAEL MEYEROWITZ & SAM SANCHEZ

ILLUSTRATIONS BY NATASHA LESSNIK

Allworth Press New York

Published by Allworth Press, an imprint of Allworth Communications, Inc., 10 East 23rd Street, New York, NY 10010.

Distributor to the trade in the United States and Canada: North Light Books, an imprint of F&W Publications, Inc., 1507 Dana Avenue, Cincinnati, OH 45207. To order additional copies of this book, call toll-free (800) 289-0963.

Book design by Michael Meyerowitz
Illustrations: Natasha Lessnik

Library of Congress Catalog Card Number: 89-81077

ISBN: 0-927629-06-2

The Graphic Designer's
Basic Guide to the
Macintosh®

BY MICHAEL MEYEROWITZ & SAM SANCHEZ

ILLUSTRATIONS BY NATASHA LESSNIK

Acknowledgements The authors gratefully acknowledge the following for their help: Apple Computers, Inc., and other Macintosh hardware and software manufacturers, for providing current product information. Barbara Harkins of Harwood Publishing and Design for copy-editing assistance. Edward Brown, publisher of *Computer Buyer's Guide and Handbook,* for help with photo research. Special thanks to Jolynne Miller, Richard Di Lorenzo and Tom Nimblett.

Toolbox *The Graphic Designer's Basic Guide to the Macintosh* was produced on Macintosh SE and II computers. Text was written in Microsoft Word 4.0. Page layouts were assembled using QuarkXpress 2.12. Original illustrations by Natasha Lessnik were created with Illustrator 88.

Fonts used include Adobe's Franklin Gothic family and New Century Schoolbook, which was condensed in QuarkXpress. Page and chapter numbers were set in Emigre Ten, a digital typeface by Emigre Graphics.

Artworks shown throughout the book were created in the respective programs. Screen shots were taken using Capture by Mainstay, and ImageGrabber from Sebastian Software. Some photos and images were scanned for position only with Dest's PC Scan 1000 and 2000 scanners.

Pages were proofed on an Apple LaserWriter NT and camera-ready layouts were produced on a Linotronic 300 Imagesetter at Microcomputer Publishing Center in New York City.

Contents

What to expect

PART I

Introduction

Revolutionary technology for graphic design

The invasion was inevitable. We had already grown used to seeing their little glass faces peering at us in airports, banks, and libraries. Personal computers were even invading our homes. People used them to process words, to spew out never ending spreadsheets, to play electronic games.

Eight years ago, graphic design companies that had personal computers probably used them in the accounting department. Creative types found no artistic allure in those early machines. But all that has changed. There's no longer any question that the personal computer has become an important force in the graphic design industry. Designers must confront the brave new world of electronics because the revolutionary technology they've been waiting for is here, now. And, because personal computers will affect all phases of the design cycle, it's important to venture in thoughtfully and deliberately.

Personal computers owe everything to miniaturization. The first computer, ENIAC, developed forty-five years ago at the University of Pennsylvania, weighed in at 30 tons. Today, powerful microprocessors encoded on tiny silicon chips allow personal computers to digest twice as much information and retrieve it with lightning speed.

The seeds of revolution

The original Macintosh with mouse and keyboard. Add-ons included the ImageWriter dot matrix printer, external disk drive, numeric keyboard, a modem, and carrying case.

Steve Jobs and Steve Wozniak built the first Apple personal computer in a garage in Palo Alto, California, in 1976. The new product did so well that companies like Tandy and Commodore began developing their own machines in anticipation of the public response that was to follow. IBM's entry into this market legitimized the concept of personal computers and set a standard that aroused the interest of other powerful players like Xerox, Hewlett-Packard, and Texas Instruments. As the technology became more widespread, more and more companies entered the market.

But Apple was at a disadvantage. Its computers cost as much or more than IBMs or compatible machines and they lacked the power and hard disk memory needed to make them attractive to business users. The Apples didn't have the internal "umph" to crunch complex numbers or run sophisticated word processors. Another deterrent to quick success was Job's desire to create a simple "closed" computer – outside developers couldn't add additional features to the basic machine. In spite of its slow start, Apple continued making refinements and adding features.

Welcome to Macintosh With the introduction of the first Macintosh in 1984, Apple began to close the gap between itself and its competitors by offering a user-friendly interface packaged in increasingly powerful machines. Before the Macintosh, personal computers were all code-driven – commands had to be typed in a specific sequence. One typing error and you were stopped dead in your tracks.

The Macintosh, with its dowdy, cream-colored plastic shell, may have looked like the low-tech step-sister of the industry but there's no denying that it revolutionized the way people used computers. When you flick on a Macintosh you see a smiling computer face followed by a "desktop" where tiny file folders lie waiting to be opened with an external pointing device called a "mouse." There is no confusion with codes here, commands are on menus that pop open when you "point and click" with the mouse. And when you're through with a file, you "drag" it to an on-screen trash can.

Trash   Trash

It was the unique visual and physical interface of the first crop of Macintoshes that helped introduce computers to thousands who found code-driven machines too complicated. Mac users quickly discovered that menus are relatively consistent between different programs. The command to print in a word-processing program was the same as in a drawing program. Learning new software was faster and easier than before.

Hand-in-hand with the development of more powerful computers, Apple developed the LaserWriter, a printer that applies toner to paper at a resolution of 300 dots per inch. Apple capitalized on the creative potential of the Macintosh and the LaserWriter from the beginning. Print ads boasted the ability to mix graphic images with text in various fonts and sizes on a single page. One series of national ads displayed packaging and printed materials created for a fictitious baby food company. These early examples of the Mac's artistic capabilities signaled the new wave of technology that would create desktop publishing.

The phenomenon of desktop publishing would not have been possible without the Macintosh, the LaserWriter, and PostScript, a page-description language developed by Adobe Systems. It was PostScript that gave the Mac hardware the unique capability of turning images and text into a series of codes that allow high-resolution viewing and printing. The licensing of PostScript to software companies spurred the development of page-layout programs like Aldus Corporation's PageMaker, a package for assembling a complete publication on the Macintosh. Once all the ingredients were in place, Mac users began creating pages where body copy automatically flowed from column to column, where graphics were sized and cropped on screen, and where type could be enlarged up to 127 points.

Business bites the Apple

With the Macintosh and the LaserWriter, Apple had unwittingly created the basis for the first inexpensive graphic workstation with immediate business applications. Firms that were staunchly devoted to IBM-compatible machines began taking another look at Apple's computers. Many purchased Macintoshes for the express purpose of creating business presentations and internal publications. The growth of desktop publishing technology gave rise to a flood of newsletters, magazines, and books. Suddenly, anyone with a Macintosh and a LaserWriter could become a publisher, and many did.

Graphic designers found these early systems too primitive. There was no color, no high-resolution output, few typefaces, and despite the 300-dot-per-inch capabilities of the LaserWriter, the technology lacked the precision needed for critical projects.

Designers also saw the early desktop technology as a threat. People with Macintosh computers, they contended, were elbowing into design because they knew how to use drawing and page layout software. Rather than assimilate the technology, many designers chose to ignore it and continued working with traditional methods.

Design meets technology

What many designers failed to realize was that technology would march on. It wasn't long before Macintosh files found their way to high-resolution imagesetters like the Linotronic, the same type of machine that typesetters use to produce galleys for traditional publishing and design. Systems whose screen representations are vastly superior to anything designed previously for desktop publishing are appearing in computer stores. And slick features that software developers couldn't consider incorporating into their programs before are now possible. Adding to the flood of technology is the development of IBM-based software for drawing and page layout.

The computer as a design tool is an evolution whose time

has come—for the uninitiated there's a lot to learn. It's important to know where to start since the marketplace is flooded with electronic options. Tools like scanners, modems, and color printers are all a part of a system that is rapidly replacing traditional studio methods.

Graphic designers are aesthetic specialists. Their training and background give them a visual sensibility that is well-suited for working with the Macintosh's "icon"-based interface. There are many designers who use other computers but, if given a preference, most will choose Apple's Macintosh over all.

In 1989, *MacWeek,* a computer industry weekly, commissioned a market study that polled graphic designers from the American Institute of Graphic Arts as well as subscribers to *Art Product News* and *Step-by-Step Graphics.* The results showed that one out of three graphic arts professionals uses Macintoshes for graphic design, and 12 percent use IBM PCs, PC compatibles, or PS/2s. Two-thirds of those questioned predicted greater use of Macs in the future. Another study by Diagnostic Research, Inc., commissioned by Apple Computer, clearly indicates that Macintosh has significant advantages over code-driven machines in a number of areas, including productivity, reduced training costs, ease of installation, and quality of the finished product.

These are indeed confusing times for graphic designers. The language of bits and bytes, of RAMs and ROMs, can present obstacles to achieving a complete understanding of the new electronic design cycle. The only way to demystify computers is to learn more about them. The information in this book is meant to help those who are curious and ready to explore the new computerized Macintosh studio. Making the transition from pencils to pixels won't be easy, but the rewards will be well worth the effort.

Why Macintosh for design?

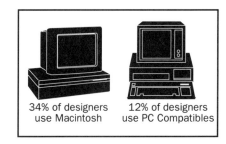

34% of designers use Macintosh   12% of designers use PC Compatibles

Take a byte

Getting started

Who's got time
for computers?

CHAPTER 2

Have you ever noticed how small design studios always seem to bustle with activity? That's because the designer/owner usually takes on the dual role of creative force and business manager. These double responsibilities leave little time for extras when you throw in client meetings, going on press, and collecting past due accounts. Anticipation of the time that will be taken from a frantic schedule in learning to use a Macintosh computer is enough to prevent many designers from considering it at all.

Even when time is not an issue, graphic designers with traditional art school training have no experience that prepares them for today's electronic design process. Then there's the cost of purchasing a system. It's no wonder that designers are left feeling unsettled by the industry's transition to computers and are overwhelmed by the thought of learning how to use them. What they fail to realize is that the Macintosh is just another tool. It may seem intimidating but it still takes the designer's creative input to make the magic happen. Learning the subtleties of what hardware and software can produce takes time but it is not impossible .

The transition to designing on a Macintosh should be planned so it doesn't disrupt the studio work flow. The process involves more than just a few weeks. A perfect example of the gradual incorporation of the Macintosh into the studio process is the in-house design department of Milton Bradley, maker of Monopoly and other popular board games. Designers there began by using the computer to create simple layouts for game rules and score sheets. There was no pressure to move on to bigger things until everyone had learned the basics. No job deadline was ever compromised by the computer. Today, Milton Bradley's designers happily point out that entire projects—packaging, game boards, and cards—are produced on the Macintosh.

Unmasking the mystery

The best way to begin learning about the Macintosh is to talk to a designer who uses one. Local graphic arts organizations, Macintosh user groups, and computer retailers are good places to find designers who are willing to share their experiences. Design and computer magazines can also be helpful. Don't be put off by ads filled with technical gobbledegook. The articles are generally written in plain English so that even if you don't understand a word or two, you'll get the general idea. Some magazines even have "how-to" sections written especially for beginners.

Sometimes, the best way to get the necessary information is to delegate the task to a designer on your staff who may be enthusiastic about working on the Macintosh. When someone on the creative team takes the lead, it's easier for everyone else to join in gradually.

Advice from an expert

Hiring a computer consultant to help ease the trauma of transition is not as expensive as you might think. Purchasing the wrong hardware can sabotage your plans and cost more money in the long run. The right consultant will not only understand the technology but will also possess in-depth knowledge of the graphic design business. By seeing how your business operates, a consultant helps you look at the "big" picture and recommends the appropriate technology.

Talk to other designers who've been in your predicament. They can help identify the right consultant for your needs. Be warned that the field is totally unregulated, so a consultant's reputation is an important factor to consider. You must feel confident that the expert you choose is qualified to recommend a Macintosh system that will deliver the design and graphic capabilities your studio requires.

Consultants usually work on a project-based contract or on an hourly fee basis. Any contract you sign should define exactly what the consultant is expected to produce. Be sure to include specific objectives and the agreed-upon amount of payment. When you negotiate an hourly fee, ask the consultant to give you a weekly report of what has been accomplished and how long it has taken to do the work. Regardless of which method of payment is used, all specifics should be addressed in detail and in writing. As with any contract, have your attorney look it over before you sign on the dotted line.

In your search for a consultant you may come across value added resellers (VARs) who, unlike consultants, charge no outright fees. Instead the cost of their services is built into the price of the hardware and software they sell you. Be warned that VARs are often locked into the product lines carried by the companies they represent. This may or may not be a good thing, depending on your particular needs. If you start with a VAR and then have to switch to a consultant, the cost could be high.

Don't expect the success of your studio's transition to Macintosh technology to fall entirely on the consultant's shoulders. As in any cooperative arrangement, both sides have responsibilities. As the client, you should have a clear perspective of the benefits you expect. And even though it's precious, you will have to make time for the consultant to meet with you and your creative staff to discuss the necessary details. In the end, no consultant's work is worth it if you don't have a serious commitment to act on the advice you're given. If the consultant's report ends up in a binder on a bookshelf, it hasn't done its job.

Class action   Some graphic designers prefer to become acquainted with Macintosh technology by taking an electronic graphic design course. It sure beats those long hours spent pecking at a keyboard and trying to make sense of an instruction manual filled with jargon. There are computer design courses offered all over the country. Some classes are run by art schools and colleges, others are available through Macintosh users' groups and professional organizations like the Graphic Artists Guild. Many computer dealers and service bureaus offer courses as well. Retailers sometimes offer overview courses that are low on in-depth information but serve to give you a basic look at a typical Mac system.

Find out about a school's reputation before you sign on to take a class. What do other graphic designers think of the courses offered there? Select a school that isn't also in the business of selling hardware or software. This ensures that your teacher is more interested in your particular needs than in pitching products. No matter where you take a class, make sure the instructor has a background in art and design. Ask to see samples of design work if you have doubts. It's also a good idea to examine the equipment you'll be using in the classroom. A course is useless if it's taught with out-of-date hardware and software. And how much you learn can be limited if you're not assigned your own computer, or if the class doesn't include time to work on your own.

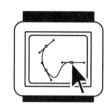

Self-help

For many, there's an exciting sense of gratification that comes with going out, buying a computer, locking themselves up in a room, and mastering the machine. Macintosh makes it easy since there's no additional hardware add-ons needed to run drawing, painting, and page-layout programs. And every Macintosh sold comes with a "Guided Tour" disk that takes you step-by-step through the various procedures needed to begin learning graphic design programs.

Bear in mind that software manuals are difficult to follow and often have to be supplemented with third-party publications, videotapes, and other tutorials. Still, with the Macintosh's interface, you'll find similarities in almost every program. Once you've mastered one software package, the next becomes easier to learn.

The hands-off approach

You may decide that no amount of classroom training or personal instruction will ever successfully convert you into an electronic graphic designer. But don't despair if you still want to take advantage of Macintosh technology. Electronic design, like other artistic disciplines, can be purchased from outside design studios or from independent free-lancers. To find an electronic board person you should look in the usual places—user groups, local design publications, etc. A well-qualified candidate will be familiar with current hardware and software and understand the graphic design process.

Electronic free-lancers usually charge an hourly fee that can

fluctuate from $25 to $100 per hour depending on what the local market will bear. Most maintain their own hardware or can work in your studio if it's equipped with a Macintosh. With the latter arrangement, you get quicker turnaround and the added bonus of being able to watch someone else use the equipment. Design studios often retain Macintosh free-lancers on a short-term basis as in-house computer trainers.

In the end, having someone else work the computer for you should be considered a temporary measure. Electronic graphic design is here to stay and graphics professionals everywhere are going to be using the technology more and more in the future. Failing to learn the basics will put you at a competitive disadvantage.

Designer's checklist: Getting started

■ The best way to learn more about the Macintosh is to talk to a designer who owns one.

■ Design and computer magazines can also be helpful.

■ Hiring a consultant to help you make the transition to computers may not be as expensive as you think. Consultants work on a project-based contract or an hourly fee.

■ Designers can become acquainted with the technology by taking an electronic graphic design course. Courses are available through art schools, colleges, Mac user groups and retailers.

■ Some designers start using the Mac on their own, learning by trail and error, and supplementing their self-instruction with third party publications, instructional video tapes, and other tutorials.

■ Electronic design can be purchased from outside vendors who charge $25 to $100 per hour.

How different is it?

CHAPTER 3

The basic order of the graphic design cycle remains essentially unchanged when using the Macintosh. The biggest differences are reflected in the way work-in-progress is presented to the client. With the Mac, it's easier to show how a project is taking shape with laser-printed proofs. Clients no longer have to visualize the finished product from pencil sketches or marker comps. It is also easier for the designer to see quickly how changes and alterations affect the look of a layout.

A typical project
The best way to illustrate the electronic design process is to show how an 8 1/2-by-11-inch three-fold brochure was produced with Macintosh technology. Nearly every graphic designer, at one time or another, has had to produce a project like this using traditional methods. In this case, the client wanted a quick, attractive, and most of all, economical solution for a two-color direct marketing mailer. Turnaround time for this project was one week.

Step one: text
Designers with Macintosh computers can ask clients to deliver copy on floppy disks. Since most businesses today have word processors and personal computers, the request isn't a difficult one to fulfill. Disks with formats that are not readily compatible with Macintosh machines can be converted with

The electronic design cycle

**Client signs
purchase order**

**Your method of working
will depend on the types
of raw materials you
receive from your client,
as well as your own
preferences and habits.**

Text

**Text is provided
in either
manuscript
or disk form**

**Modems transfer
information between
different format
machines, but do not
retain formatting**

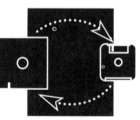

**Disk transfers
retain much
of the original
formatting**

**Optical character
recognition scanning,
good with nice clean
pages of text**

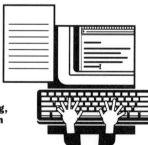

**Input text on
your Macintosh,
formatting
as you go**

Page Design & Graphics

Final Product

Page layout

Drawing original art, or reworking existing materials

Using scans for halftones, original art or reference materials

Page layout from high resolution image setter

Prepare traditional mechanicals, or output directly to film

Using laser-prints as final art

Color slides

Finished job to happy client

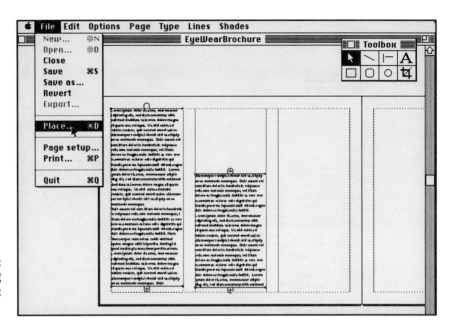

The margins and three column format for the brochure are created using PageMaker. Text created in Microsoft Word is placed into the columns.

few problems. If copy is delivered on paper, it is typed into a Macintosh word-processing program. This is done by someone on the designer's staff or a private typing service.

Since many designers don't have hardware that reads non-Mac floppy disks, they usually rely on a service bureau to convert the disk for them. Service bureaus are often offshoots of a typography business. In fact, many service bureaus started as typesetters or photostat stores. Besides converting disks to Macintosh formats, service bureaus provide high-resolution output (or repro, as it was called in the old days), color proofing, scanning of photographs and artwork, and in some cases, typesetting.

Step two: images   As with traditional methods, art and photographs can be stripped into Macintosh-produced mechanicals. Spot art and special type treatments can be created using drawing and type manipulation software, and placed electronically into the final layout. In some cases, it can be more expedient to commission a piece of electronic art from a free-lancer who produces the illustration on the Mac and delivers the work on a floppy disk.

Graphic designers often scan photographs for "position only." Scanning a photograph in a scanner converts the visual information into small dots called pixels that are transmitted to the computer. A scanned photograph never looks as good as the original. Yet, if manipulated properly, a scanned photo can

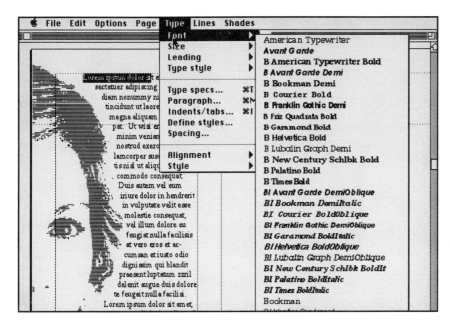

Text wrap at left is customized to conform to the shape of an image created in SuperPaint. At right, type menus allow the designer to spec the text.

be converted into attractive line art by applying screens or by adjusting the contrast. It is now possible to retouch black-and-white photographs or alter color in photos from transparencies, using Macintosh technology. Image-processing and photo-retouching programs offer features that give the designer tight controls over the creation of half-toned artwork. The degree to which designers get involved in using these types of programs will vary from individual to individual. Most designers don't retouch their own photographs now but, for those who want to get involved, the technology is there.

Step three: the layout

Layouts are created using design software. Most programs let you make templates for pages that are similar, design grids for odd-sized pages, and create style sheets for typography. With some software, text can be tagged with codes so that when it's placed in the layout it appears in the correct font and type size.

Creating a layout on a Macintosh allows you to have control of elements that previously were left to outside vendors. Artwork can be enlarged and reduced without the need to make photostats. Fonts and point sizes can be changed easily without having to go to the typesetter. Rules, boxes, and other graphic elements, previously drawn by hand on traditional mechanicals, are introduced into the design right on the Mac's screen.

A rough version of the brochure is ready to show to the client. The image of the woman's face was created from a scanned photograph that was later painted with a horizontal pattern in Super-Paint. The special type effect at right was designed in LetraStudio. The photograph of the eyes was scanned and put into the layout for "position only."

Step four: the mechanical

In the typical design process, the final layout approval is usually made from a comp. In the Macintosh studio, the client will see the layout fairly close to finished before it even goes to press. This is possible because of the laser printer.

When a project is considered ready, the final mechanicals are produced on high-resolution imagesetters, the same machines that give us camera-ready typesetting galleys. Once a design reaches this stage, the final product can be specified on film or photographic paper complete with crop marks. Color layouts can be color separated and include registration marks. It's even possible in some cases to transmit the entire job via modem directly to a printing plant.

Designer's Checklist: Electronic design cycle

■ The basic order of the graphic design cycle remains essentially unchanged by using the Macintosh. The biggest difference is that work-in-progress looks more finished than with traditional methods.

■ Designers with Macintosh computers can ask clients to deliver copy on floppy disks. Non-Mac formatted disks can be converted with few problems.

■ Service bureaus convert disks, provide high resolution repro, scan photos, and provide other computer-related design services.

■ Spot art and special type treatments are created using drawing and type manipulation software.

■ Scanned photos can be used for "position only" and stripped into the layout using regular methods. They can also be altered with special paint programs that can adjust the contrast and apply line screens.

■ Page designs are created using page layout software. Creating a layout on a Macintosh lets you have control of elements that previously were left to outside vendors.

◙ When the layouts are finished, the final copy is produced on a high resolution imagesetter.

What is needed?

CHAPTER 4

Graphic designers must answer two questions before they purchase a Macintosh computer system. The first is: What do I want to do with the computer? The second: How much can I afford? Bear in mind that even though the Macintosh is more expensive than its non-Apple counterparts, it's easier to learn and simpler to teach others to use. In a busy studio, that alone is an incentive.

Finding a balance between needs and affordability is difficult but there are ways to be clever on a budget. Mac systems can be purchased with an eye toward expandability. Extra memory, larger monitors, and additional peripherals, like scanners, can be added easily to a basic system later on. A good rule is to buy the fastest machine you can afford even if you only plan to start with simple projects. This assures growth potential for the system.

No matter which Mac system you purchase, you're going to need software to make the magic happen. Your hardware should be powerful enough to run your most complex programs. This operating power is called random access memory (RAM). Designers and illustrators who want to use sophisticated photo retouching and illustration software should be aware that this kind of software requires a minimum of two megabytes of RAM. Page layout, drawing, and type manipulation programs

The Apple Scanner and a Mac II. Flatbed scanners like this can be a real asset to the design studio. It scans artwork and with the right software it will scan text so that it does not have to be retyped.

have minimum power requirements as well. It is possible to upgrade your system's RAM later on if you find you have not purchased enough.

It's best to decide first which software packages you want to use. Then, choose the hardware accordingly. For example, most Macs come with a standard 1 Mb RAM. This is barely enough for graphic designers, who should have at least 2 Mb if not 4. With 1 Mb you will still be able to run software but response time is slower. You should have realistic expectations about the trade-offs you make by buying lower-powered machines. Choose wisely; an uninformed decision is risky.

Little extras There are other factors to consider when assembling a system. Variables like portability, speed, and expandability have varying degrees of importance to different designers and to the different types of projects they undertake and require individual decisions. A computer system is more than a screen with a keyboard. There are other components that help make up the total package. Luckily, for those on a budget, many of the following add-ons are available from third-party vendors at competitive prices.

Storage All programs and the documents you create have to be stored on a hard disk or on floppy diskettes. Graphic design and illustration documents require ample storage space. A simple project could easily fill several diskettes, so a hard disk is essential. Most Macintoshes are available with internal hard disks or an external hard disk can be purchased separately. Without a hard disk, the Macintosh performs more slowly, and all work created on it has to be saved—sometimes piecemeal—on diskettes. Without a hard disk your Mac will need a second external floppy disk drive in order to work properly.

Monitors The Macintosh Portable, Plus, and SE display only black-and-white screen dots or pixels. Designers who want to see their layouts in color will have to equip their Mac with a color or gray-scale video monitor. For business graphics, presentations, black-and-white images, and many design programs, a monitor that displays 256 colors is enough. For color retouching and color illustrations, a more powerful monitor with enhanced color capabilities is needed.

Output devices There's no way of getting around it, if you're serious about using the Mac for graphic design, you need a PostScript laser printer. Even though its resolution is only 300 dots-per-inch, the laser printer is an essential proofing tool. Once again, you must ask yourself, what are your needs? How much you pay for a laser printer is based on its speed, memory capacity, and font capabilities.

Studios with ample budgets might consider other output devices like color laser printers, film recorders that make slides, and high-resolution imagesetters.

Input devices One of the Mac's strongest features is its ability to receive information from a variety of sources. The mouse, a pointing and drawing tool, is the first and most basic input device you will need. Every Mac, except the portable, comes with a mouse. Third-party vendors make a variety of sophisticated mouse-like products with different features. You can even get digitized tablets with electronic pencils for drawing by hand directly into the computer. One device, the trackball, functions as a mouse without having to be moved about the desktop.

Another important input device that's of special interest to graphic designers and illustrators is a scanner. With a scanner, you turn artwork and photos into digital images that can be altered, traced, and used as a source of artwork in layouts. Some scanners also come with an OCR (optical character reader) that scans typed or printed text into a word-processing format, a handy feature for nontypists. A scanner is not absolutely essential, but eventually you'll probably want to have one in the studio.

Communications Time is money these days, so it might be wise for designers to consider having a modem and communications software. With the modem you can receive text directly from the copywriter, send completed jobs to a service bureau, or even show work-in-progress to clients with compatible systems. Additionally, services like MCI Mail, Prodigy, and CompuServe tap into a vast network of services and electronic bulletin boards. There are even special boards that can be installed in a Mac so that it can send and receive fax transmissions.

Configuring a system The chart on page 30 shows sample configurations of Macintosh design systems. Estimated costs are based on "street" prices, since most retailers offer discounts. However, shop around as prices will vary from retailer to retailer. Reputable mail-order houses can offer the best prices for software. These systems are based on one computer. If you add other work stations to the basic system, it will increase your overall cost, depending on the computer, monitor, and software you choose to add. Items don't need to be purchased all at once; however, those marked with an asterisk should be a priority.

I can get it for you retail In an industry that's growing by leaps and bounds, computer salespeople have a poor reputation indeed. Despite this, buying a computer through a retail store has its advantages. It's easy to see and work on the equipment and ask questions. If the machine breaks down you can bring it back. For designers with little computer knowledge, a good retailer can offer personalized service and support. But there's a price for all this attention.

Since very few retail outlets offer competitive prices for Macintosh computers, the key to choosing the right retailer is service. A salesperson in a retail operation should be ready to work with you before you purchase, letting you try out the equipment and offering reliable answers to your many questions. If you can, search out a shop that will let you make an appointment to see the different Mac models at work with the kind of software programs you intend to use.

Service should continue after you buy the system. Before you buy, inquire about warranty, training, and service. Make sure the store is authorized by the manufacturer to repair its equipment. Are repairs done on site or sent out? It could take days longer to fix your machine if it has to be shuttled to a remote location. Ask to see the repair department if possible. Does it look fully staffed and well organized? Will your retailer let you have a "loaner" for free or at a nominal cost if your machine breaks down?

Those who want more personalized service than a dealer can offer might consider hiring a consultant or a value-added retailer. As we mentioned on page 15 these professionals are equipped to assess your needs and help you get started on a Mac system.

Post haste

Many people find that it's less expensive to buy computer equipment through the mail. Computer magazines and newspapers often contain numerous computer ads that boast lower prices and special services. In most cases, these companies can offer a better price since they don't have the high overhead of retail storefronts. But buying a computer long distance means you don't get to see it in action before you buy it and you won't have a salesperson to answer your questions. You have to do all your research on your own and you get no assistance in physically setting up your system. And if your hardware needs to be repaired, you'll probably have to ship it back. In the long run, the cheaper prices are offset by the personalized service you can get from a dealer.

Let me lease

Design studios with little extra cash can consider leasing a computer system instead of buying one. Benefits frequently cited include some insurance against equipment obsolescence, tax advantages, and preserving your available credit (if you don't pay cash) for other business purposes.

In general, a lease involves a long-term contract that usually lasts 12 to 60 months, financing, and an option to buy the equipment at the end of the contract. Many leases are designed to let you upgrade the equipment as new models come on the market, but that option makes the rate more expensive. Still, for many, leasing is easier than trying to sell old equipment to pay off a loan, and negotiate new financing to pay for new equipment.

Sample Systems Possible configurations for different budgets. Add the cost of another computer and software for each additional user. Prices shown are approximate – by shopping around you can save as much as 30-40 percent.

	$3,000 – $6,000 System	$7,500 – $10,000 System
Computer	$1,300-2,500 Macintosh Plus or Macintosh SE*	$2,500 Macintosh SE*
Memory	$0 1 Mb RAM (included)	$125 additional 1 Mb RAM
Keyboard	$200 SE-Apple extended or third-party extended* (included with a Plus)	$200 Apple extended or third-party extended*
Monitor	$0 Included	$1,000–1,500 Black and white 15-inch portrait monitor*
Storage	$300–400 Internal 20 Mb hard disk*	$500 40 Mb internal* floppy disks for backup
Printer	$300–600 ImageWriter II or equivalent dot matrix printer *	$3,500–4,000 LaserWriter NT or equivalent 300 dpi PostScript printer*
Fonts	$100 Set of screen fonts purchased from a service bureau	$100 35 fonts are built into PostScript printer (set of screen fonts)
Input devices	$500 Mouse (included), hand-held scanner, or rent scanner time at a service bureau	$1,600 Mouse (included) and 16 grayscale scanner
Software programs	$1,000–1,500 Word processing*, paint/draw*, page layout*, and HyperCard (included with computer)	$2,000–2,500 Word processing*, paint/draw*, page layout*, PostScript drawing, type manipulation, telecommunications, database, and HyperCard (included)
Utilities	$100 Backup software (use hard disk backup included with computer), font management, and screen saver	$200 Backup software (use hard disk backup included with computer), font management, screen saver*
Telecommunications	$ 0 None	$250 2400 baud modem
Misc. Expenses	$ 350 AppleCare for computer*, surge protector*, and floppy disks for storage and backup*	$350 AppleCare for computer*, surge protector* and floppy-disks for storage and back up

Items marked with an asterisk are recommended hardware and software which should be purchased first. Others can be added on as the need arises.

Sample Systems

$10,000–$20,000 System

$4,500
Macintosh IIcx*

$500
4 additional Mb of RAM

$200
Apple extended or
third-party extended*

$1,700
13-inch color*
24-bit color board*

$500
40 Mb internal*
floppy disks for backup

$3,500–4,000
LaserWriter NT or equivalent
300 dpi PostScript printer*

$2,000
35 fonts are built into PostScript
printer, additional fonts

$2,500
Mouse (included)
256 gray scale scanner,
digitizing tablet

$2,500–3,000
Word processing*
paint/draw*, page layout,*
PostScript drawing*, type
manipulation*, B&W Image
manipulation*, telecom-
munications, database, and
HyperCard (included)

$ 250
Backup software , font
management*, screen saver*, and
graphic/retrieval program

$ 250
2400 baud modem

$ 450
AppleCare for computer*, surge
protector*, and floppy-disks for
back-up

$20,000–$35,000 System

$5,000–6,000
Macintosh IIx or IIci*

$775
7 additional Mb of RAM

$200
Apple extended or
third-party extended*

$5,000–6,000
19-inch color monitor*
24-bit color board*

$1,500
80Mb internal*
Tape or removable for backup

$4,000–4,500
LaserWriter NTX or equivalent*
($8,000) Color PostScript printer

$10,000
Hard disk containing
full set of fonts

$4,000
Mouse (included)
color/gray scale scanner*,
digitizing tablet

$3,000–4,000
Word processing*
paint/draw*, page layout,*
PostScript drawing*, type
manipulation*, color image
manipulation*, telecom-
munications, database , and
HyperCard (included)

$250
Backup software*, font
management*, screen saver,
and graphic/retrieval program

$250
2400 baud modem

$700
AppleCare for computer*, surge
protector*

Computer
Memory
Keyboard
Monitor
Storage
Printer
Fonts
Input devices
Software programs
Utilities
Telecommunications
Misc. Expenses

Taxes may be a factor to consider, depending on the type of lease you have. Sometimes, long-term leasing eliminates the need for depreciation of equipment because lease payments are treated as an operating expense. If you plan to deduct these payments on your income tax returns, the lease terms must fall within Internal Revenue Service guidelines.

Guaranteed in writing   Most hardware comes with at least a one-year warranty. Until recently, Apple's warranty was only 90 days. The company's thinking was that failures occurring after 90 days are so rare that a longer warranty period would not necessarily be beneficial to clients. That line of thought has changed. All Apple computers now have a one-year warranty that can be extended with the yearly purchase of AppleCare. Other companies offers extended warranties as well. Recently, credit card companies have been using warranties as promotional incentives for cardholders. You may not need to purchase an extended warranty right away if your credit card company offers such protection beyond what's offered with the machine.

Designer's checklist: Researching a system

■ Designers must answer two questions before they purchase a Mac. The first is: What do I want to do with the computer? The second is: How much can I afford?

■ Mac systems can be purchased with an eye toward expandability.

■ The hardware you purchase must be powerful enough to run the software you plan to use. This power is measured in how much random access memory (RAM) the machine has. Most Macs are sold with 1 megabyte of RAM. Designers should try to purchase a machine with 4 to 8 megabytes. RAM can be upgraded later.

■ Peripheral hardware for your Mac includes: hard disk storage, exterior monitors, a laser printer, and input devices like digitized tablets.

■ Scanners turn artwork into digitized images that can be altered, traced, or otherwise enhanced. Some scanners can read text using optical character reading software (OCR).

■ Buying a computer at retail gives you the advantage of seeing the machine and having a salesman answer your questions. The key to finding the right retailer is service.

■ It's less expensive to buy a computer through a mail order company but there's no one to help you decide which machine and configuration you may need.

■ For many designers, leasing a Macintosh protects them against equipment obsolescence, provides some tax advantages, and preserves available credit for other business purposes.

What to expect

CHAPTER **5**

First things first

Most people think that when they buy a computer they get a screen, a keyboard, and all the necessary cables. This is not always the case. Apple's computers frequently require the purchase of cables to connect printers and other components to the central processing unit. Keyboards only come with the Mac Plus. And the only Macs that have a built-in monitor are the Plus, the SE, and the SE/30. When you make a decision about which system you want, make sure to find out exactly what you're going to get. Be sure to ask what additional cables will be needed. Do not feel that you have to purchase Apple cables, as they are more expensive than third-party cables that do the job just as well.

When Apple talks about their computers they're referring to a central processing unit (CPU) or the "brains" of the machine. In the case of the Mac Plus and both of the SE lines, the CPU is packaged together in one case with the monitor. With the Mac II line, the CPU stands independently, much like the amplifier in a stereo system. Monitors and keyboards are components added on to the main unit. Each Mac has one or more expansion slots that lets you configure your system to meet your present needs and to provide flexibility for future technology.

All come with system software, demo disks, and HyperCard,

a software erector set for building your own information management programs. They all support 3 1/2-inch disks, which are evolving into the industry standard. All new Macs, except the Plus, come with high density SuperDrives that accept floppy disks with a storage capacity that exceeds the original disks used on older Macs.

Macintosh Plus

Expandability: No internal slots.

Screen/Monitor: Built-in, nine-inch, black-and-white screen.

Keyboard: Included.

Disk Drive: One internal 800K disk drive. (Shown with 800 external drive, not included.)

Memory: Comes with 1 Mb, expandable to 4 Mb.

Weight: 16 lb.

List Price: $1,799
(Often discounted below $1,200.)

Macintosh Plus A semi-portable computer for entry-level computing, this is the last of Apple's closed "architecture" machines. In other words, adding an internal hard disk or large screen is possible, but it is not officially supported by Apple, which may affect your warranty. This computer is relatively slow, but because of its low price, it makes a good second computer for word processing and simple page-layout projects. Purchasing a used Mac Plus system with an ImageWriter is one way to get your feet wet for a little more than $1,000.

Macintosh SE

**Expandability:
One internal slot.**

Screen/Monitor: Nine-inch, built-in, black-and-white screen; an external monochrome monitor can be added.

Keyboard: Not included (shown with Apple standard keyboard)

Disk Drive/Hard Disk: 1.4 Mb FDHD drive, options include 20 or 40 Mb internal hard disk.

Memory: Comes with 1 or 2 Mb, expandable to 4 Mb.

Weight: 17 to 21 lb., depending on configuration.

List Price: $2,569–$3,369 depending on configuration.

Macintosh SE This is the first compact Mac to include expansion options. It offers the user the ability to add on a larger screen or to add an accelerator board to speed things up. This machine also offers the option of a second disk drive. Though early SEs came with 800K drives, they now come with Apple's FDHD SuperDrive that offers 75 percent more storage and allows you to transfer data files between the Mac and other computer systems. The SE comes with the choice of two optional hard disks. It holds onto the original Mac tradition of a small desk "footprint" while adding refinements found in other new models. Earlier SEs had a loud internal fan, but newer models are much quieter. The SE is a good "starter" machine. The fact that you can add on monitors and hard disks makes it an inexpensive way to enter Mac computing. You can choose to purchase Apple's internal hard disk or save some money by choosing a third-party's hard disk. The SE is about 20 percent faster than the Plus.

Macintosh SE/30

Expandability: One internal slot.

Screen/Monitor: Built-in, nine-inch, black-and-white screen, external color or black-and-white monitor can be added on.

Keyboard: Not included (Shown with Apple standard keyboard.)

Disk Drive/Hard Disk: 1.4 Mb FDHD drive, options include 40 or 80 Mb hard disk.

Memory: 1 or 4 Mb, expandable to 8 Mb.

Weight: 21.5 lb., depending on configuration.

List Price: $3,869–$5,569, depending on configuration.

Macintosh SE/30 Deceptively compact, in the same casing as the SE, the SE/30 includes the new 68030 microprocessor that makes this model as much as four times faster than the SE. Earlier Macs used the 68020 microprocessor. This new addition means that when you make a change on the screen or change a number in a spreadsheet, the time it takes for the screen to "refresh" itself or for the number to compute will be that much quicker. The SE/30 also adds an additional coprocessor for faster ciphering of complex math functions. All of this power doesn't come cheap. So, unless you need a compact all-in-one package, consider the Mac II line, which offers more versatility. The SE/30 includes a sound generator useful in multimedia presentations.

Macintosh IIcx

Expandability:
Three internal slots.

Screen/Monitor: Not included.
(Shown with Apple 21-inch, two-
page, monochrome monitor.)

Keyboard: Not included.
(Shown with Apple
extended keyboard.)

Disk Drive/Hard Disk: 1.4 Mb
FDHD drive, options include
40 and 80 Mb hard disk.

Memory: 1 or 4 Mb standard up to
8 Mb (virtual memory supported).

Weight: 14 lb.

List Price: $4,669–$7,069

Macintosh IIcx The Macintosh IIcx is shaping up as the star of the Macintosh line. Smaller than the II and the IIx, the IIcx has only three expansion (NuBus) slots, which is more than enough for most users. The components are modular and come apart into five pieces for easy servicing. You can add a board for a monitor and still have room for an internal modem as well as an accelerator board. Like other Macs, you can add up to 8 Mb single inline memory module (SIMMS) of memory, which will be expandable to 32 Mb when 4 Mb SIMMS becomes available. It also has the new 68030 microprocessor. This means it's not only faster than the original Mac II, but it already contains a "paged memory management unit." It will run Apple's new system 7.0 software allowing for true multitasking. This new system also offers virtual memory which allows the hard disk to be used as extra memory, allowing you to open extremely large graphic files without having to purchase expensive Random Access Memory chips. This is an excellent machine for people who don't need the extra slots found in the Mac IIx. With a single-page display sitting on top of it, The IIcx is a sleek, handsome machine any designer would love.

Macintosh IIci

Expandability:
Three internal slots.

Screen/Monitor: Not included but comes with built-in video card for a 256 gray or color monitor. (Shown with Apple 13-inch color monitor.)

Keyboard: Not included. (Shown with Apple standard keyboard.)

Disk Drive/Hard Disk: 1.4 Mb FDHD drive, options include a 40 or 80 Mb hard disk.

Memory: 1 Mb expandable to 8 Mb.

Weight: 14 lb. without monitor.

List Price: $6,269 - $9,169, depending on configuration.

Macintosh IIci The fastest of the Macintosh computers, the IIci shares the same casing as the IIcx. This is a state of the art machine – but you will pay a premium to get this new technology. It has only three slots but costs $1,000 more than the IIx, which offers six slots. While this machine is designed for serious number crunching, its speed is a boon to graphic programs, which also utilize its fast performance. This speed is generated by a second microprocessor that makes the IIci perform up to 45 percent faster than other computers in the Mac II line. There is also an optimal memory cache card that can accelerate this computer further still. The IIci includes a built-in hookup to a gray scale or basic color monitor. If you want more than 256 colors, you'll still have to add a video-board.

Macintosh II

**Expandability:
Six expansion slots.**

**Screen/Monitor: Not included.
(Shown with Apple 13-inch color
monitor.)**

**Keyboard: Not included.
(Shown with Apple
standard keyboard.)**

**Disk Drive/Hard Disk: 800K
disk drive, options include 40 Mb
hard disk.**

**Memory: 1 or 4 Mb standard,
up to 8 Mb.**

**Weight: 24 to 26 lb.
depending on configuration.**

**List Price: $4,869–$7,369,
depending on configuration.**

Macintosh II   Though no longer made by Apple, there are thousands of these machines available through resale at reasonable prices. Whole systems including CPU, monitor, keyboard and a 40 or 80 Mb hard disk can be found for several thousand dollars less than a new IIcx. This was Apple's first open architecture machine and offers six expansion slots, which means room for everything from a "board" to run a monitor to one that can act as a fax machine in tandem with the computer. Though this computer takes up a large amount of room on your desk, it can be turned on its side to free up space. It was the Mac II that made the graphic design community first take notice as it not only offered an easy way to add a large monitor, but was the first machine to support color. This machine offers stereo sound capabilities.

Macintosh IIx

Expandability:
Six expansion slots.

Screen/Monitor: Not included.
(Shown with Apple 13-inch color
monitor.)

Keyboard: Not included.
(Shown with Apple
extended keyboard.)

Disk Drive/Hard Disk: 1.4 Mb
SuperDrive, optional 40, 80, and
160 Mb hard disk.

Memory: 1 or 4 Mb standard
up to 8 Mb.

Weight: 24 lb.

List Price: $5,269–$8,569

Macintosh IIx A new generation Macintosh II, this computer includes the newer 68030 processor, a coprocessor that speeds math functions, and the SuperDrive. Not as fast as the IIci, this machine is still poised for the future, supporting Apple's plans for its next generation of system software. It is a good machine for an individual who may want to add several boards internally. Because of its larger size, the IIx has room for larger full-height internal hard disks. It comes in several configurations and supports the AUX operating system, which is Apple's version of the UNIX operating system. This opens the Mac up to several programs that run on work-station level computers.

Macintosh IIfx

Expandability:
Six expansion slots.

Screen/Monitor: Not included.
(Shown with Apple 13-inch color
monitor and monitor stand.)

Keyboard: Not included.
(Shown with Apple
extended keyboard.)

Disk Drive/Hard Disk: 1.4 Mb
SuperDrive, options include 80,
and 160 Mb internal hard disk.

Memory: 4 Mb standard
up to 8 Mb.
4 Mb DRAM kits available

Weight: 24 lb.

List Price: $8,969–$10,969

Macintosh IIfx The newest addition to Apple's line blurs the distinction between personal computer and workstation. The same size as the II and the IIx, this machine is twice as fast as the IIci. Though untested in the marketplace at press time, this machine promises to deliver state-of-computer performance. It is based on the 68030 processor with an added coprocessor and memory subsystem. It has a static RAM cache which stores frequently used data, allowing for an instantaneous response in many procedures. Another new feature includes an input/out subsystem, speeding up the sending and receiving of data between computer components. All of these features add up to incredibly fast graphic imaging on screen. This computing power and new technology doesn't come cheap. The Macintosh IIfx is obviously designed to take full advantage of Apple's new operating system due in the Summer of 1990, and will serve as a model for future high-end computers from Apple.

Macintosh Portable

Expandability: Limited.

Screen/Monitor: Built-in, additional black-and-white monitor supported.

Keyboard: Built-in.

Disk Drive/Hard Disk: 1.4 Mb SuperDrive, optional 40 Mb hard disk.

Memory: 1 or 2 Mb (static RAM).

Weight: 16 lb.

List Price: From $5,799.

Optional: Numeric keypad, modem, video adapter, and battery charger.

Macintosh Portable Introduced in late 1989, the long-awaited Portable weighs in at three pounds less than a Plus or an SE. This puts it more in the "luggable" class. Costing over $6,000, this machine doesn't come cheap. It is the only battery-operated Mac (lasts about six to ten hours before recharging). It uses a trackball instead of a mouse, but its keyboard is standard, so you miss out on the function keys. Though the Portable adds several innovations, it is ironically closer to the old SE in terms of operation than the newer Mac II line. If you must have a portable to lug to clients, this is the only Mac game in town. Otherwise, wait until this category gets a few more players.

Surge protectors Computers are fragile machines. They shouldn't be manhandled or subjected to fluctuations in electrical current. A "surge protector" stops surges of electricity that can cause the Mac's central processing unit to lose data or damage internal hardware. There are different types and models of surge protectors. Some look like electrical strips used in kitchens to hook up several small appliances. Cheaper models may not offer the same protection a more expensive unit can give. Some of the high end models come with warning lights and buzzers that signal when too much surge activity is taking place.

Accelerator boards An accelerator board can help if you find yourself spending too much time watching the Macintosh screen redraw itself when you make a change. Accelerator boards for the Mac are usually manufactured by third party vendors. They are installed inside the computer in one of its expansion slots. Accelerator boards give the computer a hand in speeding up serveral functions. The price tag is expensive but the results are amazing. A good accelerator board can take a slow Mac Plus and make it into a quick and nimble SE/30.

Tilt and swivel Staring at a computer screen all day long can give you a pain in the neck. So things like tilt and swivel devices can make all the difference. There are wall-mounted brackets that can get the computer off your desk and allow you to swing it out of the way when you don't want to use it. Keyboards can be stashed in special drawers that mount on the underside of your desktop and slide out when you want to work.

Designer's checklist: The basic components

■ Apple computers require the purchase of cables to connect components to the central processing unit.

■ Keyboards only come with the Mac Plus. And the only Macs with built-in monitors are the Plus, SE, and SE/30. All others require the purchase of a separate monitor.

■ Each Macintosh has one or more internal expansion slots that let you configure your system to meet your present needs and provide flexibility for future additions.

■ All Macs come with system software, demon-stration disks, and HyperCard software. All new Macs, except the Plus, come with high density SuperDrives that accept floppy disks with a storage capacity that exceeds the original disks used on older Macs.

■ A surge protector regulates surges of electricity that cause the Macintosh to lose data or damage internal hardware.

■ Other Mac accessories include accelerator boards that speed up the computer's performance.

CHAPTER 6

I can see clearly now

One of the original features that made the Macintosh so revolutionary was its built-in monochrome screen. With everything in one unit, the Mac embodied the very concept of a "personal" computer. Despite its nine-inch size, the Mac produced sharp screen images in black and white. The display was like pencil or ink on paper. Critics often complained of the Macintosh's claustrophobic display. But there were plenty of others, graphic designers included, who were impressed by the screen's resolution and happy to work with it.

But size has its limitations. With the small Mac screen you can see a whole- or a double-page layout but the representations are small. Sometimes page elements get so tiny that all you see is a gray blur. To work on individual elements you must enlarge the page view and see it a section at a time. Even though it takes some getting used to, creating layouts this way is a real option for designers. In fact, before the Mac II came along, it was the only option available. Now there are monitors with portrait (tall) or landscape (wide) orientations; small, medium, and large screens, monochrome, color, and grayscale. Whatever your design needs, there's a monitor for you.

There's no denying that screens that display whole- or double-page layouts improve productivity by 25 to 50 percent

A scanned photo as it appears on screen in 1-bit (standard 9-inch Mac screen), 4-bit, and 16-bit modes.

since designers don't have to "scroll" around to view the entire contents. And being able to see designs in color is certainly helpful for a designer. But just like everything else in the Mac world, the bigger or more powerful it gets, the more it will cost. Once you've decided how much you can afford, there are other factors that come into play.

How much monitor?

When you purchase a monitor you actually are purchasing a computer "display system" that includes the monitor, a video board that is installed in the central processing unit, and software that runs the monitor. There are many manufacturers, including Apple, that make display systems for the Macintosh. Screen sizes can vary from 13 to 21 inches. The monitor you choose should be based on your personal preference and the type of work you do. You will have to stare at this glowing tube in a box for several hours a day, so pick the one that best suits your aesthetic.

Monitors work along the same principle as television sets – with a "gun" device at the back of the unit that projects signals onto a phosphor coating on the screen. These signals energize the individual phosphor dots which in turn configure and align themselves to create the screen representation. The color, clarity, and definition of what you see on the screen is all dependent on the type of phosphor coating used.

It's all in the pixels

Designers will best understand the concept of "pixels" if they think about a photostatic line screen. Photographs for newspapers are coarsely screened with fewer dots while photos screened for glossy magazines require more dots per inch. Pixels are the dots or "picture elements" that appear on a computer screen. Their number, density, and strength determine the quality of display for all types of monitors.

Display Mode	Number of Colors	
One-bit	2	colors (black and white)
Four-bit	16	grays or colors
Eight-bit	256	grays or colors
Sixteen-bit	32,768	colors
Thirty-two-bit	16,777,216	colors

Resolution Good resolution is determined by how many pixels are actually on the screen. A high-resolution monitor might show as many as 1,996,800 individual pixels aligned in horizontal and vertical lines on the screen. The square ones which Macintosh uses, and which have become a computer industry standard, produce cleaner representations since they fill the screen more completely.

Fidelity How images look on the computer screen in relation to how they look when they are printed is important. Desktop publishing techies often refer to WYSIWYG (pronounced wiz-ee-wig) or "what you see is what you get." A monitor's WYSIWYG capability is directly influenced by the density of the pixels. The Mac SE has 72 pixels per inch, which corresponds closely to what you can print on Apple's ImageWriter or LaserWriter. As screen representations get larger, they require a density of more pixels per inch in order to maintain high resolution and true-to-life appearance.

Shading The ability to see shades of gray or different colors on a computer monitor is determined by how many "bits" a pixel contains. A standard monochrome monitor has just one bit per pixel allowing it to show images in two shades, black and white. Pixels on grayscale monitors can have one, two, four or eight bits. A grayscale monitor with eight-bit pixels can display up to 256 shades of gray. Most color monitors currently sold are eight-bit systems that permit the designer to see 256 different colors. Color pixels can contain up to 32 bits and permit the viewing of 16.8 million different colors.

It's important to explore the various aspects of monochrome, grayscale, and color monitors. Which one is right for a graphic designer is a personal choice. Bear in mind the limitations of your Mac system's central processing unit. An SE, for example, may take a large screen at the expense of speed.

Monitor mania

Radius two-page monitor for the Macintosh SE/30. The obvious advantage of this size monitor is its ability to display a double-page spread at actual size.

Other things to consider include:

Size As with television sets, monitor screen sizes are expressed as diagonal measurements of the actual picture tube before it's put into a plastic casing. Since part of the screen is hidden by a frame, the exposed area will be smaller, in some cases by up to two inches.

Screen savers The phosphor coating on your monitor screen is light sensitive, but if the phosphor is energized an image can "burn" into the screen coating and leave a permanent etch. To prevent this, you use a "screen saver," a program that automatically detects prolonged inactivity and darkens the screen until you resume work. Some screen-saver programs display moving patterns, fireworks, or even a clock. Screen savers can be set to begin several minutes after they detect no activity.

Refresh rate A monitor's "refresh rate" is measured in the time it takes for the screen to redraw itself when a change has been made or when moving elements about on a page layout. "Flickering" is the result of a slow refresh rate since the eye detects the small changes in energy. For easy viewing and clear images a refresh rate of 60 hertz (Hz), or 60 times per second, is needed.

Software Sometimes monitor manufacturers provide software tools that make working with a large-screen monitor easier and more productive. Some programs let you keep electronic tools and menus on the small screen, leaving the large screen free for your design work.

Video cards Since the monitor has no real intelligence built in, the computer needs a video board in order to control the monitor. This board is installed in an internal slot in the central processing unit. As the brains of your display system, the video board is integral to your monitor's operation. With some monitors, video cards can be upgraded to give improved performance.

Monochrome monitors are not to be sneezed at. Their clean, crisp display of text and line art is perfect for jobs that don't require photos or continuous tone art. They are, however, unsuitable for design-related tasks like retouching photographs or for illustrations that require subtle shading. This is because a monochrome monitor must create the illusion of gray with a process called "dithering"—creating a dithered pattern of alternating black-and-white pixels. Pictures generally appear as grainy approximations of their originals.

Make mine monochrome

Graphic designers who generally work on one-color jobs or an occasional two-color job could easily work with a monochrome monitor. Many designers go this route and use the computer to create black-and-white mechanicals while marking color specs on overlays and stripping in photos traditionally.

Grayscale monitors are indispensable tools when retouching photographs, assembling photo montages, and creating subtle shading and airbrush effects on illustrations. If photographs play a significant part in your design work, a grayscale monitor is the most economical and efficient means of seeing them on-screen in photo-realistic detail. This is possible because on a grayscale monitor each pixel can be different shades of gray. For designers, a grayscale monitor makes sense when image quality is important but color is not cost justifiable.

Going gray

The number of gray levels a monitor can display depends on

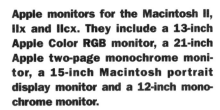
Apple monitors for the Macintosh II, IIx and IIcx. They include a 13-inch Apple Color RGB monitor, a 21-inch Apple two-page monochrome monitor, a 15-inch Macintosh portrait display monitor and a 12-inch monochrome monitor.

the amount of memory in the video card that comes with it. A one-bit (monochrome) card provides two (black and white), a four-bit card gives you 16 grays, and an eight-bit card can display 256 grays. Some video cards can be upgraded to provide more gray levels or do double duty if you later purchase a color monitor. And although photorealistic images require 256 gray levels, money can be saved if the designer can get by with four or 16 shades.

One advantage of a grayscale monitor is how smoothly it displays text. It's even better than on color monitors. Font "anti-aliasing" is a computer-generated trompe l'oeil that uses gray pixels to make the edges of on-screen letters seem smoother and more fully formed. The process compensates for built-in restraints and works hand-in-hand with grayscale technology. To reap the benefits of this technology, screens must display at least four shades of gray.

Living color   Color monitors are more comfortable to look at. The real bonus in having a color display system is the limitless design and production options it brings into play. You can instantly see how spot colors affect layouts, create color type treatments, produce color illustrations, retouch color photographs, and even generate color separations. Your every color fancy is instantly gratified.

The decision, once again, boils down to whether price or design needs affect your buying decision. Many designers make do without color. But when they can, designers will purchase color display systems even though they cost twice as much as a monochrome counterpart. A 13-inch monitor that displays 256 grays or colors is an ideal starter monitor for a designer who works on many types of color projects. It's the same size color screen that Apple first made for the Mac II in 1987.

An image that appears on a color monitor seldom matches the printed version. All you see is an approximation of the final. This includes on-screen Pantone colors. There are calibration tools that can be used to get your monitor as close to real color as you may want. But if you work on a color monitor it's best to specify a color by its Pantone number, or by a percentage of cyan, magenta, yellow, and black. Designing with a color solely based on what you see on screen is risky. However, over time, many designers learn to predict color results based on previous jobs.

Color monitors have three electronic "guns," all firing at the screen at the same time. Just like a television set, all the colors you see are created by different combinations of red, green, and blue. And just like monochrome monitors, color screens must use dithering to create the colors they display. With an eight-bit video card you see 256 colors. But now with 24- and 32-bit video cards the possibilities become almost limitless. There's no denying the dramatic difference you get when you can see 16.8 million colors.

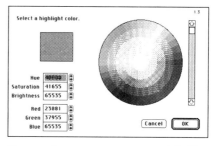

On a color screen you can pick the color of your choice to highlight text and graphics.

Designer's checklist: Monitors

■ Monitors that display whole or double-page layouts improve productivity by 25 to 50 percent.

■ When you purchase a monitor you are actually purchasing a computer display system that includes a monitor, a video board, and software.

■ Pixels are picture elements that appear on the computer screen. Their number, density, and strength determine the quality of display for all types of monitors.

■ The ability to see shades of gray or different colors on a monitor is determined by how many bits each pixel has. One bit equals two colors, four bits equals 16 colors, eight bits equals 256 colors, 16 bits equals 32,768 colors, and 32 bit equals 16.8 million colors.

■ Monitor sizes are expressed as diagonal measurements of the picture tube before its put in a casing.

■ Monochrome monitors are suitable for text and black and white line art.

■ Grayscale monitors are indispensible for re-touching photographs, assembling black and white photo-montages and for viewing subtle shading and airbrush effects on computer-generated illustrations.

■ Color monitors are more comfortable to look at. The real bonus from a color monitor is the limitless design and production options it brings into play. A 13-inch monitor that displays 256 grays or colors is an ideal starter monitor for a designer who works on many types of color projects.

Input devices

How do I get it into the computer?

CHAPTER 7

In the big, wide world of computer jargon, an "input device" is any piece of hardware that lets you communicate with the computer or transfer information into it. This encompasses a three-ring circus of devices large and small. There are digitized tablets, trackballs, microphones for digitizing your voice, and scanners in black and white and color. There's even a wireless headset that beams infrared or ultrasound signals using breath or head movements. And then of course, there's the basic mouse (eek!).

The central processing unit of your computer is like the amplifier in your stereo system – it needs input devices like a turntable or compact disc player to be able to work properly. And like a sound system, a computer can have any number of input devices attached to it. On new Macintoshes, input devices become part of a "desktop bus" system allowing several different connections. That means that a designer could easily opt for having a mouse and a digitizing tablet. Macintoshes without a desktop bus can use a special connector for hooking up multiple input devices.

A better mouse trap

They call it a mouse because it sort of looks like one. The Apple standard-issue mouse is about the size of a pack of cigarettes and has a square button that sends commands

A trackball for the Macintosh manufactured by Kensington. The track ball is like a mouse on its back. Instead of rolling around the desk, the unit remains stationary. On-screen movements are controlled by rolling the ball around in its socket.

when you "click" it. Most mouses have a ball on their underside that rolls around in a plastic casing. To make the ball roll, the mouse has to be moved around on a flat surface like a desk top or a "mouse pad," a small square with a surface designed to provide sufficient friction for the mouse to roll properly. When you roll the mouse about, an on-screen cursor makes corresponding movements. The mouse lets you point at choices from menus, lets you draw, select text and graphics, and lets you physically move elements around the screen. Most Mac users never need more than the mouse they got with their computer.

There are reasonably priced mouse alternatives for artists and designers with specialized needs. For starters, there's wireless "optical" mouse devices that use infrared light signals transmitted to the computer when it's rolled around a special optical mouse pad. Trackballs are mouses that have been turned on their backs. Instead of rolling them around, the ball is exposed and you roll it around by hand. The advantage to this is that the trackball is stationary and you gain more space on your desk. And former video game freaks will be happy to know that there are even joysticks available as Macintosh input devices.

A keyboard steps in where a mouse cannot tread. With a mouse you can point and click but you can't type your name or fill in a special point size on a type style sheet.

Tickling the keys

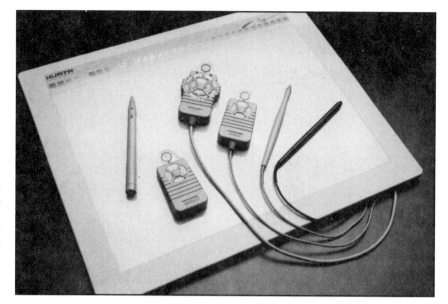

A digitized tablet by Kurta shown with a variety of drawing devices including a cordless stylus and three different styles of pucks. Though not as simple as using a traditional pencil, a digitized tablet comes close to recreating the feeling of putting ink to paper.

If the mouse is the first and most basic input device, the keyboard is the most important. Strangely enough, the first Macintosh keyboard was primitive. It was too compact for comfort and lacked "function keys" that provide shortcuts by storing long series of commands on one key. Apple's newer keyboards are desktop bus-ready and come in a roomy standard size, and in an elegant "extended" model that sports 15 function keys. All Macs also ship with a software program called Easy Access that lets you simulate mouse movements using keyboard commands.

Designers should consider using an extended keyboard. Apple's keyboards are by far the most expensive made for the Macintosh. So those on a budget might want to consider keyboards from third-party manufacturers, some of which include special "macro" software for use with the function keys. Almost every software program takes advantage of these keys. And with macro software you can specialize a key's function to suit a particular need. You'll find that the function keys come in handy once you become more proficient on the computer.

Drawing room Let's face it, the mouse is cute but it's not really a drawing tool. It's a pointing device. You can draw with a mouse but control is minimal at best. If you're going to do illustrations, you might want a digitized tablet. Though not as simple as using a traditional pencil, a digitized tablet comes close to

A ScanMan hand-held scanner by Logitech for the Macintosh Plus, SE and II. Hand-held scanners are inexpensive, easy to use, and provide a quick way of scanning small pieces of artwork.

recreating the feeling of putting ink to paper. Each tablet comes with software that controls the lines per inch and the scale of a drawing once it's in the computer. A tablet can also be used with specialized templates or overlays that activate the commands for a specific software program. One unique tablet teaches the computer to read your handwriting.

There are two things to consider when purchasing a tablet: the size of the work surface and the kind of drawing device you need. Tablets can range in size from the standard 8 1/2-by-11 inches to 18-by-24 inches. The size you choose should be the one that is most useful for the type of work you do.

Most tablets can be teamed with any number of drawing and pointing instruments. These can include the "puck," a sort of souped-up mouse with multifunction buttons and a small lens with crosshairs for accurate line control. Another device, the pen-shaped "stylus," can have one to four buttons and in some cases be cordless. The cordless stylus uses batteries that add weight and make it less comfortable for drawing.

Scanning the situation

All scanners perform the same basic task, which is to convert what they "see" into digitized dot patterns. This is similar to the process of photocopying. With a scanner, the electronic "toner" is sent to the screen via cable. Once there, it's ready to use as is, or to be dumped into an illustration or drawing program.

A good digital scanner should be at the top of your design

A Hewlett Packard ScanJet desktop flatbed scanner with a sheet feed mechanism. Having a sheet feeder on a flatbed scanner is useful especially when scanning several pages of text at a time.

hardware shopping list. If you can't get one right away, don't worry – service bureaus will scan images for as little as $10. But having a scanner in the studio offers more spontaneous design possibilities. Scanners are the electronic equivalent of a stat machine or a copier that reduces and enlarges. A scanner not only can scan line art, it can simulate halftones. Even better, scans can be placed in software that can change and enhance the image.

Since most scanners operate similarly, scanner software should be your main concern. The easier the software is to use, the more likely you are to save time and frustration. Consider again what type of scanning you will be doing. If you work mainly with photos, look for software features that help you work in that area. If you deal mostly with line art, you'll have different needs. Look around, sometimes third-party software vendors make special software for particular brands of scanners.

The best choice for a design studio is a "flatbed" scanner which, like a copier, has a glass surface where the original is laid flat. Flatbed scanners let you scan images from books and oversized originals or anything mounted on cardboard. Most of them can handle images sized at 8 1/2 by 14 inches with more expensive models being able to handle 11 by 17 inches.

The alternative to a flatbed scanner is a "sheet-fed" scanner that accepts the image through a slot and moves it through and back out again using rollers. Art on very stiff board cannot be fed through the slot. And glossy photographs have a tendency to not roll through smoothly. Sheet-fed scanners work best with images on standard weight and sized paper.

Read the resolution Desktop scanners for the Macintosh usually capture images at 300 dots per inch. This corresponds well with the 300 dots per inch that most laser printers reproduce. But for traditional printing, this resolution is too low. However, something large can be scanned and scaled down, allowing the resolution to become more dense, making it acceptable for many purposes. Another trick is to use a low-resolution scan as a template that is traced and redrawn using drawing software. This process renders a high-resolution image that's camera ready.

Many of the features you look for in a scanner are directly related to the type of monitor you work with. How many grays or colors a scanner reads doesn't matter if your monitor can only display black and white.

Black and white and gray As with monitors, scanners can reproduce a variety of grays. Unlike traditional halftone technology, which allows for various sized dots, computers use specifically sized screen dots or pixels. To compensate for this they use "cells" that can vary the color density of different spots on the pixel. The various combinations of black and white create a particular shade of gray. This process for creating digital halftones is called "dithering." You'll need a grayscale scanner with 256 shades of gray for serious halftone work. The cost of a scanner corresponds to the amount of grayscale it can provide. For those who can compromise, less grays mean less bucks spent on a scanner. Apple's scanner, for instance, has 16 levels of gray or 4 bits per pixel (dot), which is plenty for scanning "position only" photos and art.

Color The cost of a color scanner is three to four times that of a black and white one. Keep in mind that scanned color photographs take even more memory to store than their grayscale counterparts. A copy of an eight-page newsletter with a dozen color photos will fill eleven 800K floppy disks. If you're serious about working with color scans, bear in mind that the promise of color scanning is real but there are still some difficulties. Color scanners are notoriously slow. To get the most out of a color scanner, your computer system should have at least 5 to 8 Mb RAM, and you'll need a monitor with a video board that can show you everything the scanner read.

At the high end of the scanning universe are "slide

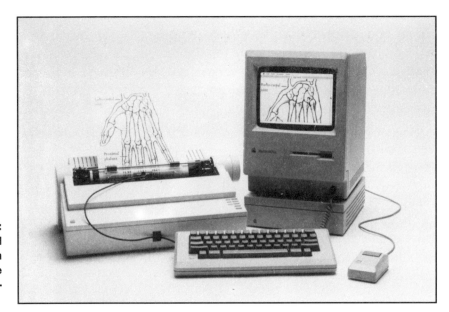

An inexpensive scanning option: Thunderscan replaces the printhead on the Apple ImageWriter with an electronic eye that reads the image as it rolls through the printer's paper-feed mechanism.

scanners" that create ultra-sharp color scans of 35mm slides, and "video digitizers" that accept video signals from a video recorder or a video camera.

If you need a scanner only occasionally, there are a couple of inexpensive scanner substitutes. Bear in mind the the tradeoffs—what you save in money will be spent in extra time used to achieve sometimes-less-than-perfect results.

Handheld scanners Scanners are small devices that can scan up to four inches across and are good for scanning small pieces of art like logos and geometric shapes. Although it's possible to join two separately scanned four-inch strips, it's a long and arduous process that isn't really worth the effort.

ThunderScan This unique product is used with Apple's ImageWriter dot matrix printer. ThunderScan replaces the print head on the ImageWriter with an electronic "eye" that reads the image as it rolls it through the printer's paper-feed mechanism. Once the image is digitized, ThunderScan lets you change and enhance it. While less expensive, scanning images this way is slower. It takes many minutes to scan a full-page image or photo using this method, all the while tying up the computer and printer. Despite this, and its awkward hookup procedure, ThunderScan is a good alternative when you only scan now and then.

Copy protection

For designers who have to turn manuscripts into computer-readable files, a scanner can act as a text-input device. Some scanners have an "optical character recognition" (OCR) capability built in and some can have it added on. Assuming you have clean copy to scan and a font that your OCR software recognizes, text can be read and transferred directly into a word-processing program. The technology has not been completely perfected. Even so, software manufacturers claim a 98-percent success rate. This doesn't sound too bad until you discover that on a page with 600 characters, that could mean as many as 12 errors. There are new OCR software packages that claim to be able to read just about any font, in any size. These programs cost about $800 and are useful tools in the right situation.

Networking party

In a design and publishing environment, networks can be time savers. Copy can go from writer, to editor, to art director, and into final layout without ever having to be printed on paper. But in a small studio, an elaborate computer network is not necessarily needed.

AppleTalk networking software is built into every Macintosh. When you hook up a laser printer to a Mac, it's AppleTalk that sends the signal from one piece of hardware to the other. A simple "network" is often a good idea if you have more than one computer and only one printer. Generally connectors run about $25 to $50 per component. But it doesn't have to stop there. Networks can get complicated and involve computers, printers, scanners, modems, and non-Mac computers as well. It's not a field for amateurs, since each component adds a new set of variables. Companies that make networking products are constantly refining and improving their products but installation can still be tricky. For complicated set-ups, a networking consultant may be a good idea.

Ring my modem

One increasingly useful input device to own is a modem. A modem, like a fax machine, uses the telephone line to transmit information. Modems are priced $150 to $500 and are rated according to the speed of data "transmission." These speeds are 1200, 2400, and 9600 "bauds." The higher-baud machines are more expensive, but you save money by using the phone line for a shorter time. It's wise to get a modem that

meets the current industry standard that is based on the modems manufactured by Hayes.

Modems are operated using software. Many come with their own software but it's better to purchase software separately so that you can pick and choose the features you want. With a modem it's possible to dial the phone, tap into "electronic" bulletin boards, or check the balance on your checking account. If you're working on a deadline, you can finish your layout at midnight, send it by modem to a service bureau, and have Linotronic output in the morning. With a modem and an internal fax board you can communicate with your client's fax machine. All of these things and more are possible with a modem.

Just the fax In some cases a scanner can be used in conjunction with an internal fax board as part of a fax system. With such a setup the scanner reads a document, sends it to the computer where it is processed by the fax board, and sent out again via telephone lines to a receiving fax machine. With this system faxes are received through the computer as files that can be transferred to paper using the laser printer. This arrangement is good for the occasional fax, but if your studio does a lot of faxing back and forth to clients, using the computer and scanner for this purpose could be counterproductive.

Designer's checklist: Input devices

■ An input device is any piece of hardware that communicates with the computer or transfers information into it. Included are: keyboards, mouses, scanners, and digitized tablets.

■ The mouse is used to point at choices on a menu, and can be used for drawing and physically moving elements around the computer screen.

■ Designers should consider using an extended keyboard with function keys that provide shortcuts by storing long series of commands on one key.

■ Having a scanner in the studio offers many spontaneous design possibilities—to scan line art, photographs or, with the right software, scan and read text.

■ Scanners for the Macintosh usually capture images at 300 dots per inch and their cost corresponds to the number of grays they can read.

■ A modem, like a fax machine, uses the telephone line to transmit information. Modems are rated and priced according to the speed of transmission (measured in bauds).

Output devices

The proof is in the printer

If your designs never had to be printed on paper you would never have need for a printer. But, alas, the promise of the paperless society has yet to arrive. One day your clients may want their annual report on an interactive disk that investors can view on a computer monitor. But for the time being, printers are necessary tools for designers who are serious about designing on the Macintosh. Printers are proofing, tweaking, and proofing-again tools. The printer shows you how your design looks when it's set to paper, and that's important for a graphic designer.

   As you investigate the many possibilities make sure that the printer you buy is totally Macintosh compatible. Make sure you know what software, cables, and wiring are needed, especially if you're not buying an Apple product. Don't expect a printer to be all things. One area where printers have trouble is printing on envelopes, odd-shaped pieces of paper, or labels. All this can be maneuvered if you persist. Sometimes it's easier to pull out the Smith Corona and type an envelope the old-fashioned way.

Dots nice

Dot matrix printers work using a print head whose quality is determined by the number of "pins" it has. The Apple ImageWriter is a nine-pin head, connected using a serial-type

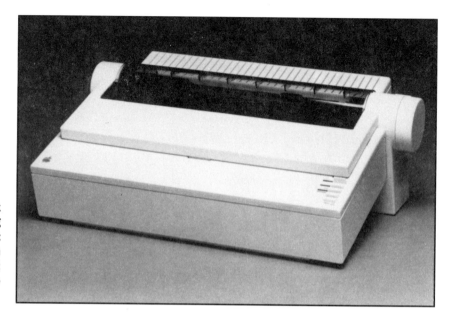

Apple's ImageWriter II dot matrix printer provides built-in color printing capability, as well as three different print speeds. It includes a built-in expansion slot that will accept interface cards for expanding the printer's capabilities.

cable. Most other dot matrix printers use a parallel cable. So be careful before replacing the ImageWriter with another dot matrix printer.

Other companies make dot matrix printers but Apple's models have special features. The ImageWriter is so named because its 72-dot-per-inch resolution matches exactly the resolution of the Apple nine-inch monochrome monitor that's on the Mac Plus and the Mac SEs. With this resolution you get "jaggies," but type and art are very readable and printouts have a low-tech charm all their own. Almost any drawing or page-layout program made for the Mac will print on the ImageWriter, making it a good tool for church bulletins, small club newsletters, and other low-budget jobs.

There are even illustrators who use the ImageWriter with black and multi-colored ribbons to create art with a modern-day, computer-etched effect. Apple also makes the ImageWriter LQ, a 24-pin dot matrix printer that accepts paper up to 15 inches wide. This machine is designed for business users looking for quality pin feed output.

One new product meant to improve the quality of dot matrix printouts and screen resolution is Adobe Type Manager. The software is designed to eliminate jagged fonts so that your screen can display typefaces of any size or style. Type Manager also enables inexpensive printers to print fonts more crisply and with less distortion. Large type sizes seem to undergo the best transformation and type at smaller sizes sometimes becomes distorted. At present, the product works only with Adobe fonts.

Dot matrix printers are workhorses. But their only place in a graphic design studio is for correspondence and billing. Some studios prefer to print their letters on a dot matrix printer because they have a more personal look than laser printing, which can sometimes appear too finished and mass-produced.

Before you can understand how a laser printer fits into the design cycle, you have to understand PostScript. When Apple first unveiled its LaserWriter it was Adobe Corporation's PostScript "page description" language that made it possible to combine text and graphics on-screen and print it out using laser technology. PostScript is also an essential component of many drawing and page-layout programs. Today it's the industry standard. Digital type vendors who used to sell only to typesetters are now transferring their typefaces into PostScript format for use with PostScript laser printers and other high-resolution machines. Soon any font you can find in a traditional typebook will be available to graphic designers with a Macintosh.

PostScript has proven so popular that several clone versions have appeared on the market. These clone languages claim to be 100 percent PostScript compatible and most of the time can live up to the claim. However, it's hard to imagine the mimicking of a computer language without losing some of its more complex functions. Alternatives to PostScript don't always work with Adobe's fonts, which are the most popular among graphic designers. However, now that other type

PostScript says it all

Type at 72 dots per inch on a dot

Type on at 300 dpi on a laser printer

Type at 1270 dpi on an ImageSetter

Type enlarged to 200 percent from an ImageWriter, LaserWriter and Linotronic Imagesetter.

ITC Avant Garde
ITC Bookman
Courier
Helvetica
Helvetica Narrow
New Century Schoolbook
Palatino
Συμβολ Symbol font for math & science
Times Roman
ITC Zapf Chancery
❀ ❏ ❀ ➡ ❀ ❞ ■ ❀ ITC Zapf Dingbats

Shown is a list of the resident typefaces that come with the LaserWriter II NTX and many other laser printers. All fonts have regular, italic, bold, and bold italic weights, for a total of 35. Other faces can be purchased and downloaded to the printer.

companies like Bitstream and Monotype are offering different versions of the same typeface, designers have a wider choice.

Software and hardware companies that develop products that work with the PostScript language have to pay Adobe a licensing fee. In an effort to break free from the monopoly that Adobe and PostScript have over Macintosh technology, Apple is planning eventually to introduce its own new and improved "QuickDraw" page description language and a separate "Truetype" font standard. Apple has promised to offer the new technology to type manufacturers free of charge, which should allow the development of low-cost QuickDraw printers that will compete with PostScript models. But don't expect PostScript to disappear. This language is the de facto standard for too many different and important components of the graphic design production cycle.

The QuickDraw connection

Laser printers that use QuickDraw technology today are not using the crispier, crunchier version promised by Apple in the future. QuickDraw lasers are less expensive but they have limited applications. They are, for the most part, designed to be low-cost machines and don't come equipped with any internal memory of their own. The computer has to calculate the way the laser puts down the toner on the page and this is a slow process.

QuickDraw printers can't do the calculations needed to mathematically scale a letterform. Another disadvantage is that drawing and illustration programs that use the PostScript language will not print to QuickDraw laser printers. Unless these printers are going to be used for a specific purpose, such as simple charts or text-only documents, they do not make good tools for a graphic designer.

At the low end of the color market are QuickDraw color printers that are inexpensive and good for color presentations since they can print on transparent film. But like their black-and-white cousins, these printers are not PostScript machines and often cause typefaces to appear jagged.

Let there be lasers

For designers, the PostScript language is the most important feature a laser printer should have. There are many choices in this category. All utilize AppleTalk, a system that allows the printer to be shared by several different computers and also serves to send the necessary information from the computer to

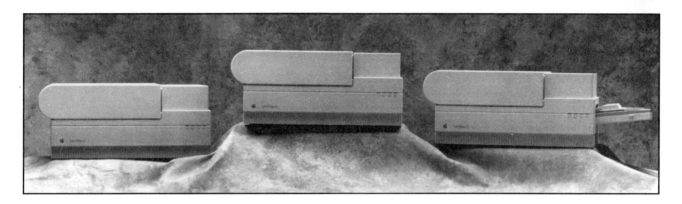

the printer's memory. Most printers come with 35 "resident fonts" (see list at left). You must purchase any additional fonts you may want to use. Higher priced laser printers have a special port that allows you to hook up an external hard disk that stores large quantities of typefaces and sends them to the printer quickly. While most laser printers have a 300 dot per inch resolution, there are some deluxe models that can give resolutions of 400 or 600 dots per inch.

Laser printers use the same basic engine, heat process, and toner that copy machines employ. Attached to the laser printer's engine is a small brain, an internal board that helps speed the process of creating finished layouts. Most lasers use expensive toner cartridges that print about 4,000 pages and cost anywhere between $100 to $130. Lately, there has been a growing trend toward recycling empty toner cartridges by having them refilled by third-party retailers. This generally saves you about half of what a new cartridge would cost.

Sitting around waiting for the printer to finish its task can be a waste of time. If speed is a consideration, you might want to consider a machine like Apple's LaserWriter NTX, which can quickly configure pages for print even when they contain several different typefaces and pieces of art. Just like a computer, a laser printer's speed and performance are based on the internal random access memory. The more RAM, the faster and more efficiently it performs. But you will pay a premium for the additional power. Some manufacturers like Apple offer upgrades for some of their laser printers, but these are expensive as well.

Make sure the printer you buy supports the brand of typefaces you like to use. And while PostScript-compatible machines have proved their muster, it's better to go for the

Apple's LaserWriter family of laser printers is based on the second-generation Canon LBP-SX printing engine. Just like a computer, a laser printer's speed and performance are based on the amount of random access memory.

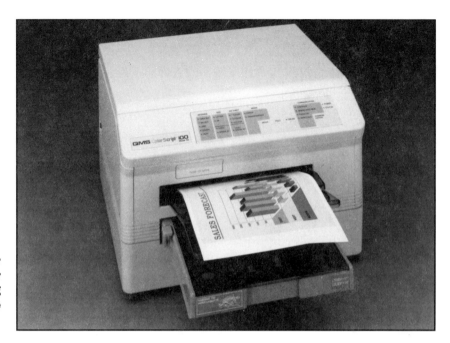

The QMS ColorScript 100 color laser printer. Although expensive, color laser printer technology is moving forward rapidly and prices are starting to drop.

real thing. There also are printer "emulators" software packages like "Freedom of the Press" that allow inexpensive printers to print PostScript documents. They do this by using the computer as the processor instead of using the one in the printer. These emulators work, but they take extra time to process before they print and, may have below-average results for documents that mix different types sizes and graphics on a page.

Most laser printers come with one or two paper trays, standard and legal size. Most lasers have a "tiling" feature that prints larger pages in overlapping sections that can then be pieced together by hand. Designers who do the majority of their work in tabloid sizes might want to consider the larger format printers which, though more expensive, save paste-up time and look better for client presentations.

It's wise to inspect the output of any printer you wish to purchase. Some printers, especially those built with the Canon engine like Apple's LaserWriters, produce strong blacks, but small type tends to fill in and appear bolder than it is. Machines with a Ricoh engine print lighter and make type look thinner but compensate for this with improved halftone quality.

A laser printer has a rated life cycle based on the number of pages it will print before its engine may start to have trouble.

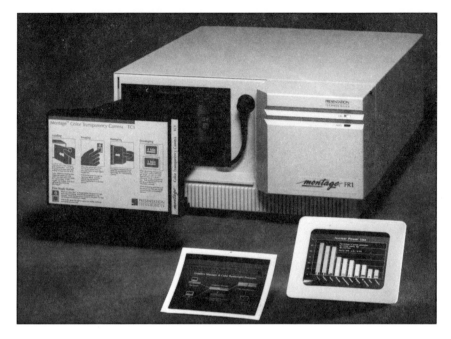

Presentation Technologies' Montage FR1 film recorder with optional TC1 camera back for creating overheads and instant prints of work created on the Macintosh.

Keep this in mind if you plan to do heavy-duty printing, such as runs of several hundred pages at a time on any given day. The average life of a laser printer is about 300,000 to 400,000 pages or about 3,000 to 4,000 pages a month.

In 1986, when Apple introduced the Mac II with its color screen, there were few, if any, color PostScript printers available. Now the field offers several choices.

Lasers of another color

As you move up the ladder to creating a full-color Macintosh studio, you can expect to pay up to $18,000 for a color PostScript laser printer. These printers work in much the same way as a traditional four-color printing press, using percentages of the four process colors. How the color reaches the paper is different from machine to machine. Howtek's Pixelmaster uses an "ink jet" process that squirts ink onto the paper. Other machines use a "thermal-transfer" process in which special paper passes four times through heated rollers to create the color.

Even though they are expensive, color lasers offer a reasonable way to provide a client with color proofs of scanned color photographs and a fairly decent approximation of Pantone colors. Bear in mind that a page printed on a color laser cannot be compared to a page from a glossy magazine. The dithered colors cannot stand up to high-quality printing presses. But the results are good enough for proofing even though the cost might run well over a dollar per page.

Sliding scales

"Film recorders" are devices used to produce slides from layouts created on a Macintosh. At present, film recorders are slow, expensive, and are just beginning to offer PostScript. Often, that means that some images do not print totally intact. Film recorders have a 35mm lens that captures the image from a monochrome monitor and photographs it through red, green, and blue filters to create the color. Manufacturers of film recorders ship software with the machines but, beware, this software is often not compatible with the presentation or drawing programs of your choice. It's a good idea to check with the manufacturer as well as a service bureau that's knowledgeable about such software.

Film recorders also come with their own set of fonts, which have to be used to get good results. Most support 256 colors, while others claim they can print up to 16.7 million. This may explain why the sharpness and brightness of colors vary from machine to machine. If you use slides only occasionally, it might be a better idea to contact a slide service bureau that can print directly with your software program, or recreate the slides from scratch on their system. Most of these services offer overnight turnaround.

The best images

The machine that made it possible for a Macintosh to stand as the front end of a graphic arts workstation is Linotype's Linotronic L100 and L300 imagesetters. The Linotronic was the first high-resolution imagesetter that printed Macintosh files on repro paper, the same medium used by typesetters for camera-ready copy. With the Linotronic, text, images, and rules are all printed simultaneously at 635, 1270, or 2540 dots per inch, the same resolutions that digital typesetting has offered for years.

A photo scanned at 300 dpi was placed in a page layout in Design-Studio where the number of lines per inch was specified in the print dialog box. Halftones were output at 1270 dpi on a Linotronic 300 ImageSetter.

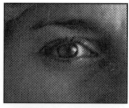
85 lines per inch

100 lines per inch

133 lines per inch

Linotronic laser imagesetters produce professional-quality text, line art
and halftones on film, paper, or
press-ready plates. The Linotronic is
one of several high-end machines
that can be used to produce camera
ready layouts.

Most design studios will continue to buy high-resolution repro, from a service bureau, but as prices drop it will become feasible for a large design studio to consider purchasing one of these machines. These are not desktop units. They contain mini-computers with large processing mechanisms and you will need a separate photo processor. Whoever operates the imagesetter must be well-trained and knowledgeable. As with all other Mac products, there are many different high resolution machines available from companies like Compugraphic, Monotype, and Varityper. All have joined Linotype in the PostScript world.

Designer's checklist: Output devices

■ Dot matrix printers work using a print head whose quality is determined by the number of pins it has. The Apple ImageWriter has a nine-pin head.

■ It is the PostScript page description language that makes it possible to combine text and graphics on-screen and print them out using laser technology.

■ A designer should have a PostScript (or compatible) laser printer.

■ Just like a computer, a laser printer's speed and performance are based on the amount of random access memory.

■ Look at a printed page before you buy. The quality of laser output can vary. Sometimes type will fill in, look thinner or bolder.

■ Other output devices include film recorders for making slides, expensive color laser printers, and high resolution machines like the Linotronic.

Electronic storage

CHAPTER 9

Make room for data

Look around your studio. There are probably a few file cabinets, flat files, and shelves where jobs and related artwork are kept. This type of storage may one day be unnecessary in the world of electronic graphic design. But one thing is for certain, storage, of the computer variety, is here to stay. The Macintosh does not automatically come with a built-in storage device. Usually, this is offered as an option. What it does have is a "disk drive," a slot that accepts a 3 1/2-inch computer disk. When a "floppy disk" is inserted into a drive, the magnetic material inside the disk receives or sends signals, i.e., information, to and from the computer.

Macintosh disk drives have gone through several changes since they first were introduced. Original Macs arrived with drives that could read disks formatted to store 400K (kilobytes) or 1,024 character units of information. These were followed by 800K drives that accepted double-sided floppy disks. The new SEs and the Mac II family of computers now sport "SuperDrives" that accept 1.44 Mb disks and read disks with data created on non-Mac systems.

Floppy basics   The floppy disk is the first and basic form of storage for computers. Software is sold on floppy disks and you'll probably store your finished design projects on them as well. Floppy

External hard disks come in all shapes and sizes. At right are Rodime's 60Plus, 100Plus, and 140Plus external hard disks. At left are two LaCie Cirrus external hard disks. Once it's hooked up, an external hard disk sits under or alongside the computer.

disks get their name from the older styled 5 1/2-inch computer disks that are pliable and easily bent. The 3 1/2-inch disks that the Mac uses are encased in rigid plastic and are more resilient than the larger ones. In spite of this, floppy disks must be handled with care. Protect them from dirt and dust, and don't let them come in contact with a magnetic field (like a portable cassette player) since this might cause the information on the disk to be erased. On one corner of the disk is a sliding lock that prevents any accidental erasure or alterations. Floppy disks are generally sold in boxes of 10 or more and include labels. A box of 10 range in price from about $15 for 800K disks to about $35 for 1.44 Mb disks.

A brand new floppy disk has to be "formatted" the first time it is put into the Mac's disk drive. This is a simple process and takes a couple of minutes. Since all Mac disks look alike, it's important to use the ones that are compatible with your computer. Using the wrong disks spells trouble and manufacturers won't guarantee their product if used in the wrong format. If you're in a pinch, it's possible to format a disk for a lower storage capacity but not for a higher one. For example, you can format an 800K disk for 400K but not the reverse.

Inside or out?

Floppy disks offer a convenient form of storage but using them exclusively is time consuming and impractical. With simple tasks like word processing, it's possible to use an external disk drive that reads your computer's "system software" while the internal drive holds the program and the document you are creating. Graphic design and drawing programs are complex

The Bernoulli box is one of several cartridge systems available that stores information on a removable disk.

and the documents created on them are large, especially when compared to text documents. It's easy to run out of operating capacity and storage space quickly with floppy disks. This is where "hard disks" come into play.

A hard disk is like an electronic filing cabinet where work is stored in files. A hard disk works like a floppy disk except that it's made of glass or metal, and coated with a magnetic substance. As it spins, the hard disk constantly sends and receives information to and from the central processing unit of your computer. But unlike a floppy disk, a hard disk has much larger storage capabilities. For graphic design and illustration work, a hard disk is essential.

Internal hard disk

One of the options when you purchase a Macintosh is an internal hard disk. Since it's installed inside the computer, an internal hard disk is a convenient and out-of-the-way solution to the problem of storage. With an internal hard disk, a Mac SE becomes an easily portable self-contained unit. On other machines, an internal hard disk is a space saver since there's one less component on your desktop.

There are many third-party vendors that sell internal hard disks for the Macintosh, generally for a couple of hundred dollars less than those sold by Apple. These third-party products should be installed by a specially trained technician, and that in itself may eat up the savings. Also, a non-Apple hard disk, is not covered by AppleCare, so check the manufacturer's warranty to see what recourse you have if your internal hard disk goes bad.

An external hard disk is a stand-alone unit, with its own power supply, encased in a high impact-resistant plastic shell. Connecting a hard disk requires a "SCSI" (pronounced scuzzy) cable that provides high-speed communication with the Mac. When properly configured, up to nine hard disks or other "SCSI" devices, like scanners, can be daisy-chained along this cable. Once it's hooked up, the external hard disk sits under, or alongside, the computer.

External hard disk

A 20 Mb hard disk can be purchased for about $450. But beware of shopping for price only. Companies come and go, and if your drive dies you'll be better off with a manufacturer with a long and established reputation.

As you shop, inquire if the hard disk comes with any extra goodies like utility programs for backup and retrieval of lost information. Other freebies could include security software for password protection of documents, or programs that "partition" a hard disk into smaller sections so that it operates faster. Some hard disks even come with "shareware," free programs written by developers for use on a trial basis. For many of these useful programs, the developer asks that you pay a licensing fee if you like the software and continue to use it. Remember that these small developers are free-lancers and rely on these small fees in order to continue developing new software ideas.

Software ideas

Talk to any designer who uses a computer and they will say these machines sometimes do strange, unexplainable things —like suddenly losing data, or freezing up, or just plain crashing. Sometimes software programs will go haywire—the Mac screen displays a bomb icon and informs you there's been a "system error." And if you think computer viruses are just for big-league machines, guess again. They really exist and can cause loss of data. Then, there's the problem of the floppy disk that was used this morning but is now deemed "unreadable" by your Mac.

Beware of the back-up blues

Hard disks can crash too. And when one does, take heed: This means all jobs, billing information, software, fonts, all

The Apple CD SC is a front-loading disk drive that reads information from specially formatted compact disks. One compact disk can hold an entire encyclopedia.

other information is lost. Sometimes this data can be salvaged using "disk recovery" software but that takes a whole day and there's no assurance that the information will be resurrected intact. The time lost recovering these files can be costly if you're on deadline. That is why it's important to "back up" the information on your hard disk from time to time.

There are backup software packages available. In fact, Apple ships one with its computers. Some software backs up information incrementally by adding only what was changed or added since the previous backup.

Backing up a hard disk is not a quick and easy task but you'll be happy you did it. To back up a 40 megabyte hard disk takes about 50 floppy disks and about two hours of your time. A more practical method is to back up your hard disk to a second one.

Info to go One of the newest storage and backup devices is a removable hard drive that vaguely resembles an audio cassette and is slipped into an external drive that transfers the information from main hard disk. Once that's done the cartridge pops out for storage. The drive costs about $1,000 and the cartridges are around $100 each—but they hold 20 or 44 megabytes of information. This type of drive and cartridge system is finding favor among designers since you can store graphic images on one cartridge, fonts on another, and client work on still another. Other backup devices include a drive that uses magnetic tape in much the same fashion as a tape recorder.

Those who work with color-intensive images might consider using an "erasable optical drive" that uses a laser disk that stores 600 megabytes. Optical drives are expensive. At present, they start at about $3,500. Another alternative is "WORM (write once read many) drives," optical drives with mega-memory storage. The laser disks using this system can be used only once and aren't erasable. They will, however, continue accepting new information until they exhaust their storage capacity. It's possible to put a whole library on a WORM laser disk. In fact, Microsoft, the software manufacturer, offers the majority of its Macintosh programs and training manuals on one single disk. Keep an eye on this technology because it will be prominent in desktop multimedia and computer training.

If you work in different locations from time to time, a good choice for you might be a "toteable" hard disk. These units weigh under five pounds and are usually small enough to fit in a briefcase. They have all you need in the way of portable storage, making it easy to hook up to the host computer.

Designer's checklist: Electronic storage

■ The 3 1/2-inch floppy disk is the first and basic form of storage for the Macintosh.

■ A hard disk for storage is essential to any system used for graphic design. Hard disks are built in to a computer (internal) or stand alone (external).

■ As you shop, inquire if the hard disk comes with any utility programs for backup and retrieval of lost information.

■ It's important to back-up the information on your hard disk from time to time. It is not a quick and easy task but it is good insurance against hard-disk problems.

■ One of the newest storage and backup devices is a removable hard drive that resembles an audio cassette and is slipped into an external drive. This type of cartridge is being used by many designers since different cartridges can be used to store fonts or large projects.

■ Laser disks provide read-only storage.

Software

CHAPTER **10**

The magic of software

File

New Folder	⌘N
Open	⌘O
Print	
Close	⌘W
Get Info	⌘I
Duplicate	⌘D
Put Away	
Page Setup...	
Print Directory...	
Eject	⌘E

The "system software" that comes with your Macintosh works like the ideal government – maintaining order, letting programs do their job, offering access to fonts, and providing "utilities" for various tasks. System software makes it possible to copy, save, delete, find, and print files. It creates the Mac's unique "desktop" metaphor, the graphic user interface that has made it so popular. System software also helps by providing "dialogue boxes" that appear on screen when a wrong or impossible command has been given. These "prompts" help guide you and make mistakes less likely.

Macintosh system software is updated and revised periodically by Apple. Company software developers make changes and refinements that often add more features to the package. You can purchase system "updates" through Apple but they are usually available free from Mac user groups and some retail outlets. Several versions of the Mac system have been released since the first machines hit the marketplace in 1984. When the new System 7.0 is released in the summer of 1990, only Macintoshes with two megabytes of RAM will be able to run it. This leaves lower-powered Macs at a disadvantage. The information that follows is based on Mac's System 6.0, the latest available at press time.

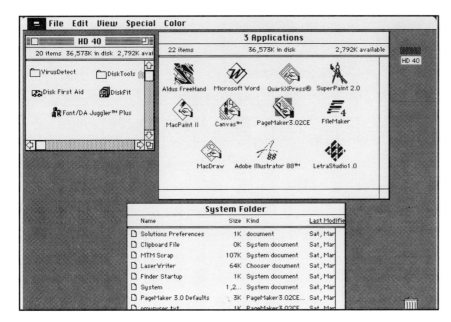

Files on the Macintosh can be viewed in three formats: small icons; large icons, or as a list that can be arranged by date, size of document, or type of application.

The System

The Macintosh functions using several different programs, each with a specialized function. Collectively these programs are the "System" and reside on the computer's desktop in a file labeled "System folder." The following is a partial list of items in the System folder and the tasks they perform.

System The system folder also includes a "System File." Only one system file should be on your start-up disk whether—its hard or floppy. Having more than one system file will cause system crashes. Many software applications come with their own system files. Be careful not to copy these on to your hard disk.

Finder This program arranges the screen into the desktop metaphor and is basically a visually oriented filing tool. The Finder works "transparently," it doesn't have to be "opened." It functions as a computer central that among other things "initializes" and ejects floppy disks, arranges information in file "folders," and starts and shuts down the computer.

The Macintosh filing system is easy to learn. Imagine a traditional manila folder. You put papers into it. You can even put another folder into it, if you want. The "folders" that you see on the Mac screen function the same way. "Documents" and "applications" (software programs) are "filed" in folders that sit on the Macintosh desktop. Every time you want a new folder, a menu on the Finder makes that "command" possible.

Document

Folder

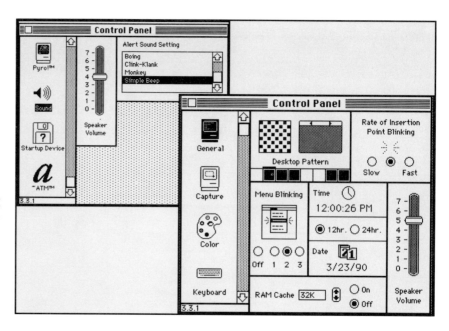

The Macintosh control panel dialog box. This is where you set the loudness of the computer's beeps, adjust the mouse's response time, and create a customized screen pattern for the desktop. Control panel devices are adjusted from here as well.

Folders can be stored inside of folders. For example, if you were working on an annual report for a client, you could have a folder named "Annual report" and inside of it have folders named "copy," "graphics," "layouts," and "contract." This method of arranging information is referred to in computer circles as the Mac's "hierarchical" filing system.

There are programs sold that replace and enhance the Finder and give it more features—such as automatically jumping from one application to another without pause, and deleting files while you're working on something else.

MultiFinder This program works with the Finder except that it permits you to open more than one application at a time. You can, for example, open a drawing and a page-layout program, and go back and forth between them without having to close either one. Using the MultiFinder takes a lot of memory and sometimes programs work more slowly than if opened one at a time. This complex tool usually works better on computers that have lots of RAM.

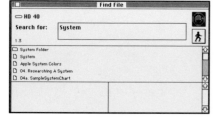

Find File The ability to store folders within folders is handy — but sometimes you forget where something is filed. "Find File" software is provided by Apple so that lost files can be found based on the letters in their names. Find File looks through all the folders and tells you where to find the document.

Trash The "trash can" sits at the lower right hand corner of the Macintosh on-screen desktop. It is used to throw away unwanted files. As long as you don't turn off the computer or open an application, anything thrown into the trash can be retrieved. After that, it is gone. The new Apple System 7.0 will require a special command that lets you review the trash before its contents are completely eliminated. If you try to throw away an important software program, a dialogue box will ask if that's indeed what you want to do. You can think it over before saying yes or no.

Franklin Gothic

Control panel The "control panel" is the software that lets you configure the features on your Macintosh desktop. It is accessed using the "Apple" menu, the little apple icon that sits at the upper left-hand corner of the screen. With the control panel's dialogue box, you set the loudness of the computer's boops and beeps, adjust the mouse's response time, and create a customized screen pattern for the desktop. There also are small, optional programs, "control panel devices" (CDEVs) that are adjusted using the control panel. They provide "utilities" like clocks, screen savers, color display adjusters, and vaccines that guard against computer viruses.

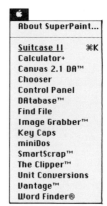
Desk accessory menu

Desk accessories Desk accessories are small utilitarian programs that can be opened no matter what else you're working on. Like the control panel, they are accessed via the Apple menu on the upper left-hand side of the screen.

Clipboard The "clipboard" is just as the name implies, a place to attach something you want to use. Since it opens in any program, the clipboard is used to copy text or images in one application and then paste them into another. Anything pasted to the clipboard must be transferred immediately, as this is temporary storage space.

Scrapbook This program stores frequently used text and images. If you're working on a letterhead design, the logo can be pasted to the clipboard and then pasted to the scrapbook. Once in the scrapbook, you can call up the image without having to go through transfer and copying procedures.

Font/DA Mover

Font/DA Mover This utility installs desk accessories and fonts

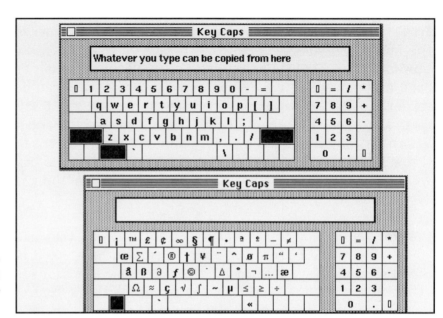

The key caps display is useful for locating the proper key for unusual characters such as bullets or international currency symbols.

into your system folder and gets them onto the Apple menu. With system 7.0, fonts and desk accessories will no longer have to be loaded with Font /DA Mover.

Key caps The "key caps" command displays a window with an on-screen keyboard showing the letters and symbols on each key. This is especially useful for locating the proper key for unusual characters such as bullets or foreign currency symbols. Key caps can be viewed in whatever typefaces you have on your system. You just choose the font. Using the mouse, you can type on this electronic keyboard and see letterforms before you use them in your designs.

Chooser The "chooser" menu lists all the different output devices hooked up to your computer, including any telephone lines used for computer communications. Most often, the chooser is used to switch to a different printer if you have more than one.

Lucky 7 When Apple releases System 7.0 many new features will be incorporated into the Mac's system software. Some were mentioned in the descriptions above. There are many changes that we can't list as yet but two in particular are important to graphic designers. The first is the "Truetype" font technology that combines the fonts for viewing on-screen with the fonts

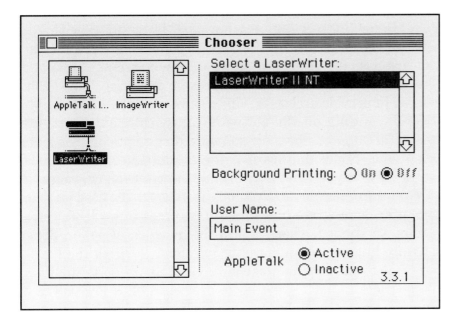

The chooser menu lists all the different output devices hooked up to your Macintosh, including any telephone lines used for communications.

used to print. At present, both types are needed. Apple says this new technology will provide true letter forms in any size, at any resolution. Important too, is the "interapplication communications" feature that lets you revise text or redraw illustrations and apply those changes universally to copies that exist in other documents.

Illustrators will be happy to know that the new system also supports "Virtual Memory." This permits unused memory on the hard disk to be used as Random Access Memory. As a result, it's easier to work on large, complex illustrations or oversized scanned halftones.

Electronic graphic design tools

No matter how important the system software is to your computer's operation, it's the applications that you'll be using for graphic design. PageMaker, QuarkXpress, SuperPaint, Illustrator—these are but a few of the programs that help designers and illustrators create their computerized work. Software programs are usually sold in a box that contains one or more floppy disks, a manual, and several "tutorials." Most applications for drawing or design cost somewhere between $200 and $500, with some layout and color products going for as much as $800.

Just like your system software, applications are revised and refined, and new versions are released. You can tell a program's "version" by the number that follows the name, e.g.,

PageMaker 3.02. A registration card is included with the software. Send it back to the company immediately. This way you are assured of getting news of new versions, "updates" that often include improved features or eliminate "bugs" that existed in previous releases. Updates vary in price from $15 to $100 depending on the software. Most companies provide "technical support" for their software on an optional basis via telephone. Some maintain it for a one-time price, others require a yearly fee that may include discounts on upgrades.

Make sure the software you buy is meant to be used on your computer. A program like Illustrator comes in an IBM and a Macintosh version. There is also the question of power. Some software has minimum power requirements. Check the box to see what these are and make sure your Mac is up to the task. It's possible to open some large programs on a low-powered machine but both will be slow to respond.

Some software is available on "demo" disks that illustrate a program's features. These floppy disks are popped into a Macintosh and give you a flavor of what the software can do. Other companies will provide the training tapes that are normally included with the software or sold separately. Either of these methods can give you a good idea of a program's capabilities without having to purchase the software. Ask around at a software store; sometimes these are free or cost less than $10. Users groups sometimes have access to demos.

Designer's checklist: Software basics

■ The Macintosh operates using several different programs each with a specialized function. Collectively, these programs are the System and reside on the computer desktop in a file labeled "System folder."

■ The Finder is a program that arranges the screen into the desktop metaphor and is basically a visually oriented filing tool.

■ The trash can that sits at the lower right hand corner of the Macintosh on-screen desktop is used to throw away unwanted files.

■ Desk accessories are small, utilitarian programs that can be opened no matter what other program is being used.

■ PageMaker, QuarkXpress, SuperPaint, and Illustrator are but a few of the programs that designers and illustrators use in their work. Make sure the software you buy is meant for your computer and be sure your machine is powerful enough.

■ Applications and system software are periodically revised and updated by their producers. Sometimes these updates are free but often there is a fee.

■ Apple's System 7.0 will include a new font technology and an interapplication feature that facilitates making changes to identical elements in different files.

■ Before you purchase software, make sure your computer has enough random access memory to properly run the program.

CHAPTER 11

Words of wisdom

One would think that aside from an occasional letter, graphic designers would have little need for a word-processing program. However, with the arrival of electronic design, more and more typesetting responsibilities are originating in the studio. Since clients provide text in a variety of media, from typed manuscripts to floppy disks, it's a good idea to be prepared to deal with a variety of formats. That means a studio should have a good word-processing program to act as the central receiving station for text.

If you get a lot of typed manuscripts, you can circumvent having someone retype the text if you have a scanner with "optical character reading" software. Scanning is a good alternative if you have clean copy, without any marks or handwriting. Once scanned, the text is then transferred to your word processor where it is proofread to ensure that all characters were properly transferred.

One common way of receiving copy is on disks that are not Mac compatible. These have to be converted into a Mac format before they can be used in layouts. The conversion can be done at a service bureau or by using a SuperDrive on a newer Macintosh. Sometimes text is delivered on a Mac disk but not in the word-processing program you have on your system. In this case, the material should be "saved" in an ASCII format, a universal code shared by all word-processing programs. But

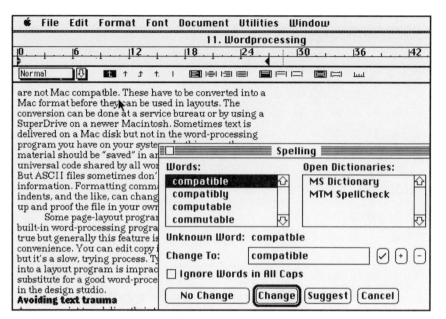

The spell-check dialog box in Microsoft Word. Most word processing programs also have search, find, and replace commands that help speed copy corrections.

ASCII files sometimes don't transfer all information. Formatting commands, such as tabs, indents, and the like, can change. You'll want to clean up and proof the file in your own word processor.

Some page-layout programs boast that they have a built-in word-processing program. These claims are true but generally this feature is offered only as a convenience. You can edit copy in a page-layout program but it's a slow, trying process. Typing huge bodies of text into a layout program is impractical. There is no substitute for a good word-processing package, especially in the design studio.

Avoiding text trauma

A manuscript typed directly into a Macintosh is the best bet. The only prerequisite is a good word-processing package, a good typist, and a good proofreader. Word-processing programs can do everything a typewriter can do and more. On a Macintosh, the on-screen text appears in the font of your choice, exactly as it will appear printed on the paper. If you specify bold or italic you see that as well. An electronic ruler lets you set type flush left, right, or centered. Word processors also let you code type so that when it is transferred to page layout it will appear in the right point size and font. Style sheets let you spec type for captions, headlines, and body copy. Most style sheets are interchangeable with style sheets in page-layout programs.

File Edit Move Notes Format Font Size Style

Free State Grill

The Free State Grill

3 Columns   Chapter 1   Page 1

Appetizers

French Fries	0.65
Basket	1.35
Onion Rings	1.95
Basket	2.65
Nachos	3.50
Potato Skins	3.45

Soup and Salad

House Salad	1.95
Chef Salad	3.95
Taco Salad	3.95
HotHouse Chili	1.75
Soup of the day	daily

Drinks

Burgers

Hamburger	2.75
Cheeseburger	2.95
Baconburger	3.45
Mushroom burger	3.25

Sandwiches

BLT	1.95
Chicken Salad	2.35
Club	2.95
Grilled Cheese	1.95
Hot Turkey	2.75
with mashed potatoes	3.25
Corned Beef	2.95
Reuben Sandwich	3.55

Breakfast

All breakfasts are served with hash browns and choice of toast

1 Egg any style	1.95
2 Eggs any style	2.55
Eggs Benedict	3.55
Cheese Omelette	3.55
Ham and Cheese Omelette	3.55
Denver Omelette	3.95
Chili Omelette	3.95
New York Omelette	4.55
(Corned Beef and Cream Cheese)	

Side Orders

Toast	0.75
English Muffin	0.75
Blueberry Muffin	0.75

A restaurant menu created using Ashtron-Tate's FullWrite Professional word processing program. Most sophisticated word processing programs have so many features that they hold an embarrassment of riches.

Often, word-processing software comes with a variety of features that are useful for studio management. One utility that many have is a "mail merge." This places names and addresses stored in a data base program on individual letters or direct mailing pieces. Word processors also have spell checkers that help with the proofing process. And "search," "find," and "replace" commands make it possible to speed through changes on large documents.

You can still go the old route and have a typesetter, or a Mac typist, "keyboard" your copy, code it, and deliver it to you on disk. The optimal solution is to let the client retain responsibility for the copy and deliver it to you, finished and complete, on a Mac disk. But, inevitably, there will be changes. Sometimes you will have to make them yourself. Text changes will be easier once the Mac System 7.0 software arrives. One new feature "links" documents, so that text corrected in a word-processing package is automatically corrected on the page layouts as well.

The original Macintosh was shipped with its own word-processing program named MacWrite. It lacked many fancy features but it certainly was easy to use. Since those times, the marketplace has splintered into a variety of niches. Graphic designers must decide what features they need, based on the most common way text is delivered by their clients.

Utilities	
Find...	⌘F
Find Again	⌘⌥A
Change...	⌘H
Go To...	⌘G
Go Back	⌘⌥Z
Spelling...	⌘L
Hyphenate...	
Index...	
Table of Contents...	
Word Count...	
Calculate	⌘=
Renumber...	
Sort	

Utility menu in Microsoft Word.

Highs and lows

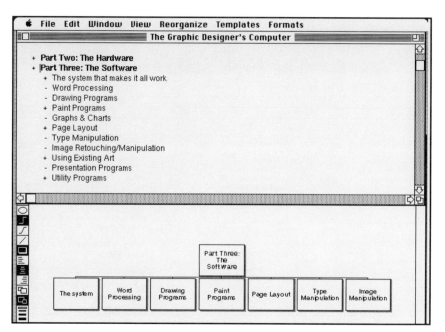

An outline and flow chart created in More. Programs like More are called idea processors because copy can be arranged in outlines, itineraries, and even 35mm slides.

In the mid-range are products that sell for around $250 or less. This includes MacWrite II, now manufactured by Claris, an offshoot of Apple. WriteNow from T-Maker, Microsoft's Write, and MindWrite by Access Technology also fall into this category. They provide a basic, sound package with limited features and work well with short documents. Often they lack extra utilities such as dictionaries, thesauruses, and tools for creating lines and boxes. Designers will find any one of these products more than sufficient for letter writing and preparing small jobs for layout.

The more sophisticated word-processing programs have so many features that they hold an embarrassment of riches. Some programs, like Microsoft Word 4.0, boast limited page-layout features. Word itself has become a standard of sorts since it has the largest base of users. It's a competent package and offers a link to other Microsoft software products, and to the company's IBM-based software. One unique feature of Word creates tables from customized parameters, eliminating the time and work it used to take to set up tabs.

Other big-league players include Ashton-Tate's FullWrite, Nisus by Paragon Concepts, and WordPerfect from the company of the same name. All have multi-column format, text-wrapping features, and "page views," an interactive, on-screen representation of the final page layout. No matter what their capabilities, these programs should by no means be used by serious designers as replacements for a good page layout program. Word-processing programs cannot accept the full array of graphic formats and lack true typesetting controls like kerning and tracking.

There are several programs that fall into unique categories— all deal with text in one way or another. Some are called "idea processors." These include programs that can make outlines from text, create daily itineraries, and let you turn lists into slides. One interesting development in this area is "hypertext." Click on a word and the screen instantly displays a definition, picture, or more information.

Other text tools include electronic stick-on notes that can be pasted on a document so that the viewer can see comments or changes. There are elaborate dictionaries and thesauruses that offer definitions and synonyms with a click of your mouse. Mini-word processors are also manufactured as Macintosh "desk accessories" that help create quick notes in any application.

Words as text and images

Designer's checklist: Text processing

■ A graphic design studio with a Macintosh should have a good word-processing program to act as the central receiving station for text.

■ Scanning text with optical character reading software is a good alternative if the copy is clean and there is no handwriting on the paper.

■ A manuscript typed directly into a Macintosh and delivered to the designer on a Macintosh disk is the best way to begin a project.

■ Page layout programs often come with built-in word processors but they are no substitute for a good word-processing package.

■ Text can be coded in a word-processing package so that when it is placed into the layout, the type appears in the correct font.

■ Style sheets in some word-processing programs let you specify type for captions headlines and body copy.

■ Microsoft's Word 4.0 has become a standard of sorts for the Macintosh since it has the largest base of users.

■ No matter what their features, high-end word-processing programs should not be used as replacements for a good page layout program.

Drawing software

CHAPTER **12**

Doodles & drawings

No matter what anyone says, working with ruling pens, French curves, and the like requires a special talent. For some designers, creative concepts fall short in the execution of finished logos and technical drawings. Droplets of ink at the corners of ruled boxes, lines with uneven weights, and inky fingerprints are all products of traditional drawing technology. Frustrating, too, is the logo that looked good in roughs but doesn't look right in the finished piece because it needs to be reworked by hand, one more time.

Having the Macintosh as a tool will not make a designer a better artist. But once the computerized drawing tools are mastered, it is easier for a designer to control the final appearance of drawings. And the designer who might have been a mediocre ruling pen artist can become a real winner on the Mac.

Drawing from experience

The earliest drawing software for the Macintosh was named, not too surprisingly, MacDraw. In its first versions, MacDraw offered the ability to draw objects that could be scaled and combined with other objects or letterforms to create type treatments, spot art, and maybe even simple layouts. The program was crude when judged by today's standards. Text handling was limited, sophisticated curves were impossible to

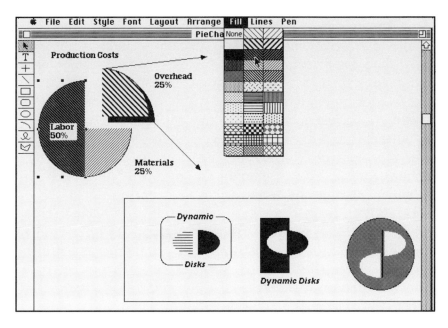

Adobe Illustrator 88™

Canvas™

MacDraw

Aldus FreeHand

SuperPaint 2.0

Work created using the original MacDraw. Though judged crude by today's standards, MacDraw offered the ability to draw objects that could be scaled and combined with other objects, or letterforms. The open menu shows the different fills available.

produce, and the thinnest weight lines seemed too heavy.

The drawing software of today gives the Macintosh capabilities not found on any other computer system. And though it's harder to master, this new breed of software can help even a novice produce some very sophisticated results. A drawing program can become an electronic sketchpad for a graphic designer. The creative possibilities expand when you work with type and free-form and geometric shapes simultaneously on the Mac screen.

While images in paint programs are read by the computer as a group of pixels or points that can be moved or changed, drawing programs are "object oriented." That means that any element, whether it be text, a geometric shape, or an image, is read by the computer as an individual boxed shape. You combine these boxes to make complex drawings. This is done in two ways. The first is by placing items in front or in back of each other and creating "layers." The other is by "joining" them together or "grouping" them so they become one object. Any individual element or groups of elements can be copied and resized. Geometric shapes can be filled with color and patterns.

Art created in drawing programs is saved in a variety of "graphic" formats. Some programs, like MacDraw, use the Macintosh format know as a "Pict." More sophisticated programs can save images in various other formats including Pict 2, MacPaint, TIFF, or EPS (see box on page 92).

Computerized tools

Drawing toolbox from SuperPaint

Most drawing programs have a "toolbox;" a set of "icons" in a small, on-screen "window." These usually include one or more "pen" tools for drawing lines, a "pointer" for selecting objects and moving them, tools for making circles and polygons, and a text tool for typing letters. Other windows along the top of the screen are clicked open with the mouse. These include a menu of "patterns" and line screens, a color selector, and menus that offer type control. The size of your drawing can be shown in inches or picas. There's usually an on-screen "ruler" that can be set so that items "snap-to" a user-defined grid. When working with large drawings, you "scroll" around the screen using the mouse to move from one part of the drawing to another. One of the best features of drawing programs are the special effects that let you slant, rotate, flip, stretch, or otherwise distort an object. And when you consider type as an object, you realize the endless potential for its manipulation into varied forms.

Many artists find the mouse uncomfortable to draw with since most drawings are created with small shapes and rules. Straight lines are easy but an arc or a freehand shape is more difficult. Many drawing programs include an electronic French

Graphic file formats

EPS (Encapsulated PostScript file) Produces sharp, high resolution images but requires a good deal of disk space. EPS files include one representation of the picture in PostScript and a representation in a PICT format for viewing on the computer's monitor.

Bitmap Images produced by paint programs. They are called bitmap because they consist of a collection of square bits that form a mosaic map of the image. The bits are represented by pixels, picture elements, on the computer screen. Bitmapped images are usually low resolution. Documents saved as MacPaint documents are in bitmap format.

PICT/PICT 2 files contain both bitmap information and mathematical coordinates for drawing high resolution images. This graphic file format is unique to the Macintosh. PICT 2 adds more formatting instructions and support for color.

TIFF (Tag image file format) are graphic file formats for use with scanners and painting programs. These formats produce high resolution graphics from photos or line art. Raster image file format (RIFF) is another format, related to TIFF created by Letraset for image processing.

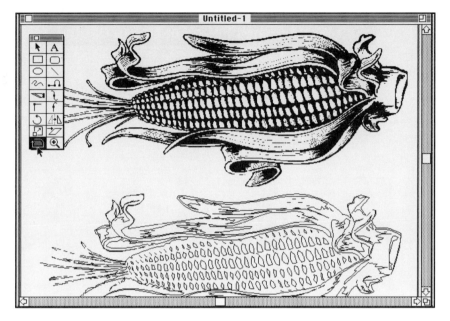

A bitmapped clip-art image by MacGraphics is placed in Freehand and traced using the autotrace command. The resulting outlined image can be used as the basis for a new piece of art. Below, a Bezier curve as it appears on screen.

curve tool that creates "bezier curves" with "points" along an axis that can be altered. It's a powerful feature, but practice is required to use it properly.

Another popular feature is "autotrace," a process that takes a low-resolution image, probably one that has been scanned, and draws over it. With a click of the mouse, you get a contour of the object. Some programs do a better job of it than others. If you need to recreate a lot of line art on the computer, consider a software package from Adobe called Streamline. This tracing program has sophisticated controls that draw outside or inside of a line and produce very effective results. Its main drawback is the $495 price tag.

There are several moderately priced drawing programs in the $200 to $400 range. They are not as complex or as powerful as the PostScript drawing programs. Other shortcomings are lack of kerning for type and lack of subtle control over patterns. However, one cannot fault these programs' simplicity since they offer a wonderful introduction to drawing on the Macintosh. Most have a relatively quick learning curve and loads of features. They are especially useful because they save and read information in a variety of different graphic file formats. This means a photo or a logo that was scanned and refined in one program might be further refined in another program with different features.

Drawing basics

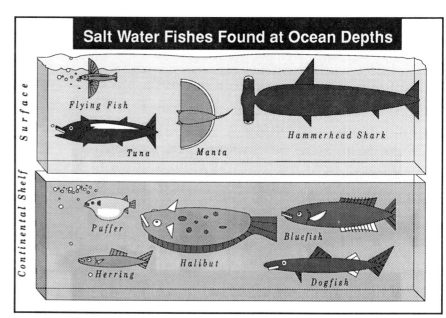

Salt Water Fishes Found at Ocean Depths

Surface — *Continental Shelf*

Flying Fish · Tuna · Manta · Hammerhead Shark · Puffer · Halibut · Bluefish · Herring · Dogfish

A color chart created using Freehand. Color is an area where high-end drawing programs shine, offering the choice of working with Pantone or the four process colors.

SuperPaint from Silicon Beach Software is a popular drawing/paint program that followed MacDraw. Images created in either a paint or a draw mode can be combined, exchanged, or saved separately. The improved MacDraw II has become a standard at many newspapers such as USA Today where "infographics" are created in full color. Canvas from Denba Software supples an array of features, including a desk accessory version that is handy when you want to create artwork while you are in another program. Other programs include CricketDraw from Computer Associates and Drawing Table from Broderbund, a new low-end package.

Powerful PostScript The drawings created on the Macintosh with Adobe's Illustrator, introduced in 1987, attracted the attention of many graphic designers. Illustrator took all the power of the PostScript page-description language and put it into an interface that appears simple but is, in reality, complex. It gives designers the kind of precision and control needed to produce exacting shapes and curves. Based on a system of "paths" and connecting "points," it lets you build the illustration, one line at a time. Afterwards, the various lines are grouped to render the final object. Illustrator also has a "template" mode that displays a faint outline of an image as it is traced. However, many of the powerful features in this program are not as easy to use as most Macintosh software. A

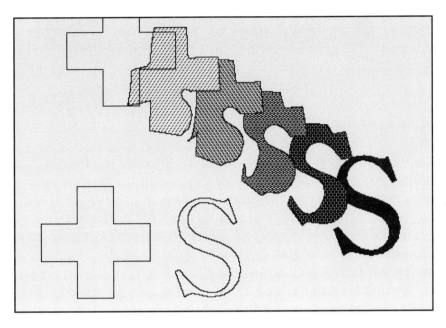

The blend tool in Illustrator lets you transform one image into another and specify the number of steps for the transformation.

lot of the power is hidden in keyboard combinations that need to be remembered, or placed next to the computer on a crib sheet.

Illustrator's chief competition comes from Aldus' Freehand, a program that uses an interface similar to the company's PageMaker layout program. Both packages are based on a system that mimics the way a designer might work on a drawing board. If you have worked with Freehand, you will feel at home with PageMaker, and vice versa.

Both Freehand and Illustrator have unique features all their own. Many designers and illustrators use both programs— Illustrator for its control over drawing, and Freehand for its ease of use and excellent type controls. Illustrator files can be opened in Freehand but Freehand files cannot be opened in Illustrator. Both programs are priced around $495.

High-end drawing programs offer the choice of saving your work in a variety of graphic images, including the "encapsulated PostScript" format that can give full-color representation when the drawing is placed in the page-layout program.

Color is an area where high-end drawing programs shine. They offer the choice of working with Pantone colors or the four process colors. Colors can be specified in one-percent

Drawing in color

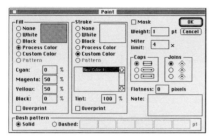

Illustrator's color menu

Gradient fill created in Freehand

increments, creating a tint that, for example, is 32 percent magenta, 56 percent yellow, and 3 percent cyan. Once the illustration is finished, a color separation can be made at a service bureau. If you're going to print Pantone colors using a four-color process, it's wise to have a Pantone Process Simulator book to give you an idea of how the color will translate.

Color drawing programs were designed with the graphic industry in mind and put a lot of the "stripping" process on the designer's shoulders. They incorporate features that deal with such concerns as color trapping; however, these are not perfected enough to offer problem-free results. Work with someone at your service bureau to make sure you won't get a moiré for misaligned screen angles. One safe way to create separations is to produce the different colors as black line art and have the printer create the screens traditionally.

Both Illustrator and Freehand offer the ability to create "gradient fills," permitting a shape to be filled with shades of a color, or colors, from light to dark, or from one color to another. With this feature, Illustrator produces a smooth transition from shade to shade. Another Illustrator option transforms one shape into another in any number of user-defined steps. For instance, an "S" could be converted into a "+" in any number of steps and you can see those intermediate shapes on the screen (see page 95).

Designer's checklist: Drawing software

■ Drawing programs are object-oriented—all elements (text, graphics, geometric shapes, rules) are read by the computer as individual boxed shapes.

■ Art created in drawing programs is saved in a variety of graphic formats including Pict, Pict2, TIFF, or EPS.

■ Most drawing programs have toolboxes that include pen tools for drawing lines, a pointer for selecting objects and moving them, tools for making circles and polygons, and a text tool for typing letters.

■ There are several moderately priced drawing programs that offer a quick learning curve and loads of features.

■ On the high end, many designers use both Illustrator and Freehand. Illustrator for its drawing controls, Freehand for its ease of use and type controls.

■ Color drawing programs were designed with the graphic industry in mind and put a lot of the color stripping process on the designer's shoulders.

Painting with pixels

Painting on a computer is not at all like putting a brush to canvas. In fact, it's quite different. Imagine a piece of graph paper as the Macintosh screen, and the paint program as a pencil that darkens boxes on the graph to create an image. On your computer screen, each of those boxes is called a pixel or a picture element. It is the basic visual unit used in painting software. On a monochrome Mac screen, the pixels can be black or white. With a gray scale monitor, pixels can be up to 256 shades of grey. And on color monitors, pixels display images with as few as eight colors, or as many as 16.7 million. (See Chapter 6 for more on pixels and monitors.)

The Mac has many levels of painting programs. Those at the high-end of the spectrum are referred to in the industry as "image processors." The simplest, like the black and white MacPaint II, are easy to use. Others, like Letraset's ColorStudio, are quite sophisticated and require patience and expertise. Finished results for these programs are quite impressive.

There are similarites in working with tools in both drawing and paint programs. The difference comes in the way the computer treats the image. In a draw program, the images are seen as one whole and complete shape. With a paint program

MacPaint II

SuperPaint 2.0

ImageStudio

Digital Darkroom

Brushing up

A black and white illustration created in SuperPaint by Charles Marcano. Several paint programs offer tools for both drawing and painting. Box above shows pixels enlarged 400 percent.

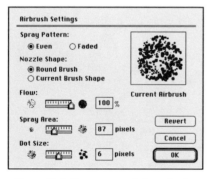

SuperPaint's spray paint controls

the computer reads an image as a group of pixels. These pixels can be enlarged on the screen, turned on or off, or have their color or intensity altered. There's a visual difference too. An image created in a drawing program has smoother edges. This is especially evident with curves and text. Illustrations created in a paint program are built pixel by pixel or "bitmapped." This tends to produce images with jagged edges.

Painting tools can create a variety of effects. Basic features include a pallete of patterns that can be altered to suit the user, pencil and paintbrush tools for drawing freehand lines and shapes, and a tool that erases parts of the image. There's a silhouetting tool that lets you separate an image from its background. And one unusual tool applies random pixels onto the screen like a can of spray paint. The text tools in paint programs allow you to type in bitmapped letters that may not be suitable for a graphic designer's needs. Future font technology is expected to relieve the problem to a certain extent. With some of the high-end programs, text is placed on a separate electronic "overlay" that prints at high resolution without jagged edges.

A complex image can often be altered in more than one drawing program. The possibilities are endless. Since many programs can both paint and draw, the two modes can be combined to get the best of each for different parts of an

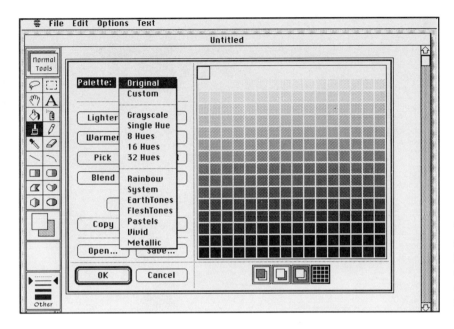

The color palette in PixelPaint. Since the introduction of the Macintosh, color paint programs have evolved into full-blown color enhancement tools with the potential of using 16.7 million colors.

illustration. A scanned photo can be placed in a grayscale paint program and retouched, or made into line art with a process called polarization. Afterwards, the same picture can be placed into a drawing program where special effects or spot colors are applied. When the process is complete, the image is ready for the page-layout program.

Less expensive, black and white paint programs cost anywhere between $50 - $200. Some even have limited color capabilities. Though they lack powerful features, such basic programs are a quick and easy way to grasp the basics of painting on the Macintosh. These programs work with images that have a resolution of 72-300 dots per inch. That makes them good tools for altering and enhancing black and white scanned images as well as line art. Paint images created in basic programs are saved in a "MacPaint" graphic format that is compatible with draw and paint programs made for the Macintosh.

Besides MacPaint, there's SuperPaint, a very popular program that lets you combine draw and paint images by layering them. Another drawing program is DeskPaint, a desk accessory manufactured by Zedcor. For designers with an eye toward the future, there's Studio 1 which includes simple animation as part of the package.

Paint basics

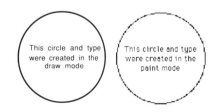

This circle and type were created in the draw mode

This circle and type were created in the paint mode

A scanned photograph placed in ImageStudio. Small boxes above show portion of image polarized with four and eight levels of gray.

Grayscale painting

Two programs that have become the standard for black and white halftone, i.e, grayscale, processing are ImageStudio from Letraset and Silicon Beach's Digital Darkroom. Both retail for about $495. These programs are unique since they have tools that can retouch or alter black and white scanned photographs. Viewing a scanned photo on a gray-scale monitor, using either one of these programs, will take your breath away. Enlarge the view and you can see the subtle shading created using the pixels.

Grayscale paint tools are unique because they can produce lines and effects that are smooth and without hard edges—like an airbrush with 256 shades of gray. Retouching photos or continuous tone art takes a lot of practice. You'll want to save your work regularly since it doesn't take much to ruin an illustration. Both ImageStudio and Digital Darkroom have "posterizing" effects that convert continuous tones into black and white, or to different shades of grays.

As good as gray scale paint programs are, they are not necessarily good enough to create first-rate halftones. The time and expertise involved in getting a decent image doesn't necessarily compete with the cost of hiring a traditional photo retoucher. Some designers may want to use scanned and retouched halftones to create comps, turning to non-computerized retouching for the finished work.

Before and after shots of photo that was retouched in Adobe's Photoshop. Image processors provide impressive tools but it takes a knowing eye to create quality work.

Color painting

Color paint programs have come a long way since the days when your best chance of getting a color image from a computer was to photograph it from the screen. Until recently color technology was there, on the screen, but there was no way to convert it to a paper print. That has changed since the arrival of color laser printers. And even though these printers don't produce true colors, they provide enough color information to give a good approximation of the finished product. Since the introduction of the Macintosh, color paint programs have evolved into full-blown color enhancement tools with the potential of 16.7 million colors. Expensive color paint programs can correct color on a photograph, strip it into a page layout, and create color separations. Original art can be scanned from a photo, a transparency or created on the screen.

The on-screen effects of color paint programs are limitless. And since each produces slightly different results, it's a good idea to test run these programs on a sample project to make sure results meet your personal design standards. When selecting a color paint program, bear in mind that there are tradeoffs. Consider software with an interface that appeals to your artistic sense. And be focused about the kind of work you expect to do. If you don't normally retouch color photographs now, do you think you'll want to do it in the future? Some of the most popular color paint programs are: PixelPaint 2.0

from SuperMac Technologies; Cricket Color Paint from Cricket Software; Studio 8 from Electronic Arts; and Modern Artist 2.0 from Computer Friends, Inc.

Paint professionals   A new breed of color image processors is now available for the Macintosh. Designed to correct color and create separations, these programs are of the same caliber as those found on high-end graphic workstations in many printing and publishing plants. These are impressive tools but, once again, it takes a knowing eye to be able to create top-rate color separations. Programs like ColorStudio, PhotoMac from Avalon Development Group, and Adobe's Photoshop offer state-of-the-art color painting and retouching tools for the Mac.

Designer's checklist: Painting and altering images

■ In a paint program the computer reads an image as a group of pixels. To create an image, pixels are turned on or off, or have their color or intensity altered. Paint images usually have jaggies.

■ There are similarities in working with tools in both drawing and paint programs.

■ Basic paint tools include a palette of patterns that can be altered, pencil and paint brush tools, an eraser, and a tools that simulates the effects of a can of spray paint.

■ Since many program both paint and draw, the two modes can be combined to get the best of each for different parts of an illustration.

■ Less expensive, black and white paint programs are good tools for altering and enhancing black and white scanned images and line art.

■ Grayscale paint programs can retouch or alter black and white photographs or other continuous tone art. These programs are unique because they produce lines and effects that are smooth and without hard edges—like an airbrush.

■ The time and expertise to to get a decent images using a Mac retouching program does not necessarily compete with the cost of hiring a traditional photo retoucher.

■ Some designers use scanned and retouched halftones to create comps, turning to traditional retouching for the finished work.

■ Since the introduction of the Macintosh, color paint programs have evolved into full blown color enhancement tools with the potential of 16.7 million colors.

■ Paint programs that boast the ability to correct color and create color separations are impressive but it takes a knowing eye to use them well.

Face to face with fonts

Type has always been an integral part of the Macintosh design arsenal. Initially, the Macintosh came with its own typefaces, knockoffs of popular serif and sans serif fonts, each named after a different city. These early efforts, while quite remarkable, were clearly not meant for use by designers. Fonts had a resolution of 72 dots per inch and printed out with jaggies on the ImageWriter dot matrix printer.

It was the LaserWriter and PostScript that made possible the first high-resolution typefaces for Macintosh computers. The first faces were basic. They included Times Roman, Helvetica, and Courier. Several more faces would follow with the introduction of the LaserWriter Plus. Apple's aim was to give business users a few choices to spruce up reports and the like. The company didn't immediately realize that it had tapped into the graphic design and typesetting stock in trade. As type technology progressed, fonts were packaged and sold like so many boxes of cereal. The first design-quality fonts to arrive on the market were from Adobe Systems, the developer of the PostScript language. Luckily, Adobe had the good sense to license quality typefaces from the International Typeface Corporation (ITC). They were expensive but good enough to meet exacting design standards.

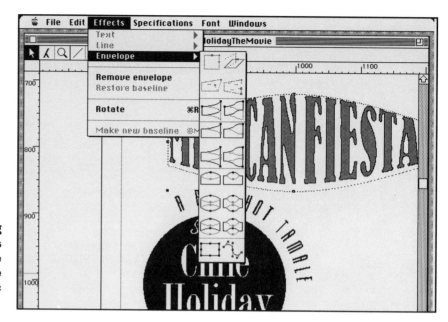

Type treatments created using LetraStudio. Open menu displays envelopes, shapes into which type can be configured. Menus below are LetraStudio type and graphic specification menus.

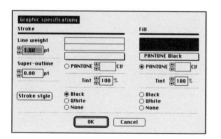

But interest from graphic designers was slow in coming. First of all, the choice of fonts was limited. Secondly, page-layout programs still lacked such type controls as kerning and tracking that could match typesetters' standards. The process of converting type to PostScript was a long, arduous task for manufacturers. Each face had to be redrawn using bezier curves and built in "hints" that help produce quality letterforms on 300 dot-per-inch laser printers. These days designers have less to complain about. Page-layout programs have added type-control muscle, and new fonts become available almost daily. There are already thousands on the shelves with many companies selling their own versions of classic faces. Designers can now agonize over which version of New Century Schoolbook is right for them.

Using fonts in a PostScript format lets you produce type in standard point sizes or in fractional increments that can go up to 999 points in some page-layout programs. PostScript faces are machine independent. As long as the printing device has PostScript or a compatible language built into it, fonts will print with excellent results. This holds true for laser printers with 300 or 400 dot-per-inch resolutions, as well as high-end printing devices that render 2540 dots per inch.

Fonts are usually sold in families of four faces. Adobe, for example, sells Goudy Old Style, Goudy Old Style Italic, Goudy Old Style Bold, and Goudy Old Style Bold Italic together as a set. When you buy a font package, you get a floppy disk that

Type treatment created in TypeStyler. With a Macintosh, a designer can stretch, rotate, or condense type using type manipulation software.

contains a computer file for each typeface in each weight. Some of the files are "screen fonts" used for monitor display and low-resolution printing. Others are "printer fonts" that are used for printing in resolutions from 300 to 2540 dots per inch. The rest of the files contains data that offer control over spacing and line breaks for each font. A package of fonts usually costs between $140 and $400. Prices have come down, as more fonts become available from different manufacturers. Some companies' bargain fonts can be purchased for under $100, but beware. You should see a complete printout of the face in order to determine if it meets your needs.

It is also possible to purchase typefaces in bulk. Some companies offer their entire line of fonts on a hard disk that's ready to hook up to the designer's laser printer. Some of these hard disks can hold over 400 fonts and cost around $10,000. Another font format that's gaining popularity is the compact disk. Image Club offers 600 brand-name typefaces on one compact disk for $5,000. For another $600, you get an external drive that reads the laser disk.

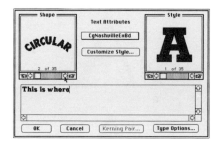

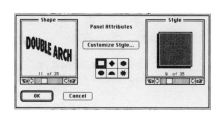

Fonts for all

Screen fonts are bitmapped versions of a font that correspond closely to the Macintosh's 72 dot-per-inch display. To get the best on-screen resolution, the proper screen font in the proper size must be installed in your system folder. If you are working with 16-point type, for example, and you only have 12- or 14-point screen fonts installed, the 16-point type will

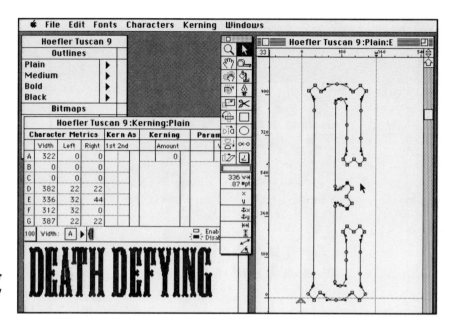

Kerning and type outline windows for Tuscan 9 typeface designed by Jonathon Hoefler using FontStudio.

Jagged screen type, above, is smoothed using Adobe Type Manager

appear jagged. However, it will print as smooth letterforms on a PostScript printer.

You can purchase screen fonts without having to purchase expensive PostScript printer fonts. In fact, screen fonts are often sold inexpensively by service bureaus and Mac-user groups. The design process is slightly altered using this approach. When you design a layout using a screen font, letters appear clearly on screen and print out bitmapped on the laser printer. Though rough, you still get a good approximation of how the design will look. The file is then taken to a service bureau that has the printer font, and the layout is outputted as final repro. There are many bitmapped fonts available as "shareware" from Mac-user groups and from other software distributors. Adobe Type Manager is a software program that enhances a font's on-screen display and renders smoother letters on dot matrix printers. With Type Manager, letters look smooth on screen, no matter the size.

Printer fonts are files that hold all the information a printing device needs to draw the type at high resolution. Without them, you can't get typeset-quality documents.

Apple's soon-to-be-released "Truetype" font technology will make working with type easier in two ways. First, typefaces will appear smooth on screen, no matter what size they are. Secondly, fonts can be printed in high resolution on laser printers that don't have PostScript. The Truetype font standard may cause confusion at first but in the end, the competition will certainly bring lower font prices with it.

Designing type

Soon after the Mac was born, Altsys, a software developer, introduced Fontastic Plus, a program designed to create bitmapped font alphabets. Much like a paint program, each letter or symbol is created using an existing font or from scratch. Each character is then placed in an alphabetical slot that corresponds to its traditional place on a keyboard. There are also programs for designing new fonts using PostScript. Fontographer, also from Altsys, FontStudio from Letraset, and Type Designer I from Kingsley ATF Corporation are software packages with powerful type-designing features. Even if you don't create an entire alphabet, these programs offer you all the tools you will need to produce clean, one-of-a-kind, high-resolution letterforms.

Until recently, a Macintosh system could only accommodate 256 fonts, 128 of those reserved for Apple faces. This, of course, became a problem as more and more fonts became available. The lack of "slots" caused confusion when using typefaces that were not in the original 128 styles, since fonts were forced to share one slot. And this, in turn, caused problems at service bureaus where the wrong fonts began appearing on final repro. These problems have been resolved with Apple's NFNT numbering system. Approximately 16,000 font slots are now available and typeface developers must register with Apple to get their own unique number.

Type around the bend

It's obvious that Macintosh technology is having a visual impact on today's graphic design. Type along curves or around circles is popping up in magazine layouts, brochures, ads, and annual reports. Many programs literally turn type into silly putty. With a Macintosh, a designer can stretch, rotate, or condense type manually. Shadows, patterns, and color can be added as well. As amusing as some of this might be, such exotic type treatments are bringing up the question of whether or not these techniques violate a font's design integrity. This is where a designer's talent and training come into play.

LetraStudio by Letraset and TypeStyler from Borderbund are two programs designed to create special effects using display typefaces. With LetraStudio, the designer uses Letraset display typefaces that are digitized versions of the company's dry transfer lettering that designers have been using since 1967. LetraStudio also has built-in anti-aliasing technology that produces crisp, sharp type at any size. LetraStudio retails for around $495 and each extra font sells for $75. TypeStyler is priced at around $200 with extra fonts sold in groups at varying prices. Freehand and Illustrator both offer many type-enhancement features, although neither program has as many features as LetraStudio and TypeStyler.

Beware of stylish type

Plain
Bold
Italic
Underline
Word Underline
~~Strike Thru~~
Outline
Shadow
ALL CAPS
Small Caps
Superscript
Subscript
Superior

Built into just about every Macintosh program is a type "style" menu for scaling text to any size, making it bold or italic, and for adding special effects like drop shadows. When letters are altered using this menu, the computer mathematically calculates the new appearance. The results are a good representation but not accurate. Today, it is generally agreed that it is best to use the manufacturer's version of an italic or bold from the font menu rather than altering it with the style menu.

Another style menu option that's not recommended is the small caps. In most Mac programs, the computer uses two sizes of type instead of true small caps that match the weight of the uppercase letters. This is being rectified with the development of small cap editions of popular fonts. Finally, most Macintosh fonts don't include characters for typing odd-fractions like 1/3 or 7/8.

Designer's checklist: Type manipulation

■ Using fonts in a PostScript format lets you produce type in standard point sizes and fractional increments up to 999 points in some programs.

■ PostScript faces are machine independent. As long as the printing device has PostScript or a compatible language, the fonts will print with excellent results.

■ Screen fonts are bitmapped versions of a typeface that correspond to the Macintosh's screen display. Printer fonts are used for printing in resolutions from 300-2450 dots per inch.

■ Fonts for the Macintosh are usually sold in families of four styles such as bold, regular, italic, and narrow.

■ You can use screen fonts without purchasing expensive PostScript printer fonts if you have your work output at a service bureau.

■ With a Macintosh and the right software, a designer can stretch, rotate, or condense type.

....

No more razor blades

It is the page-layout program where the many different elements of the electronic design cycle come together. Text, illustrations, and photographs are combined with rules, line screens, and spot color to complete the electronic mechanical. Learning to create layouts on the Macintosh takes time and patience. Once the learning is accomplished, the designer will find that working this way beats the old cut and paste methods that employed rubber cement, razor blades, and T-squares.

In their infancy, page-layout programs did not offer features that were good enough for use by most serious graphic designers. Their most obvious flaw was the lack of typographic controls. These programs, however, were more than adequate for use by businesses in the preparation of internal reports, proposals, and contracts. Others found they were perfect for small jobs such as menus, flyers, and small newsletters. Macintosh owners and Fortune 500 companies quickly adapted to the technology, and desktop publishing was born. For many designers desktop publishing signaled that nonprofessionals with technological skills were moving into design-oriented territory. In reality, desktop publishing helped create a market for professional-looking business documents. It was never meant to replace the precision design standards needed for an important project like an annual report or a slick print ad campaign.

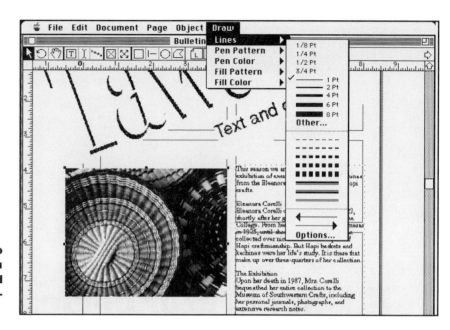

Layout produced in DesignStudio with text on an angle. Open menu shows choice of line weights and variations. Shown below is Design-Studio's type specification Menu.

Desktop publishing vs. graphic design

Technological advances today have carved out two levels of page-layout programs—the first for business publishing and the other for graphic design. Many of the original layout programs, like PageMaker from Aldus, have evolved into full-fledged design tools. Other simpler, less feature-oriented packages for non-designers continue to appear as well. Many of these desktop programs have special features like Ragtime, which has built-in data base capabilities. Others in this category include Personal Publisher from Silicon Beach Software, Springboard Publisher from Springboard, Ready,Set,Go! from Letraset, and QuarkStyle from Quark.

It is in the second, or higher, level of page-layout programs where graphic designers will find the specialized features that a professional needs. Tight text kerning, hyphenation controls, and color separations are now a part of the three major players in this field: PageMaker, QuarkXpress from Quark, and DesignStudio from Letraset. There are other high-end programs that designers employ for specific tasks. Interleaf Publisher touts special capabilities for technical documents. There are even programs designed to help create advertising layouts. These include: AdSpeed from Digital Technology; Multi Ad Creator from Multi Ad Services, Inc.; and AdWorks from Concept Publishing Systems.

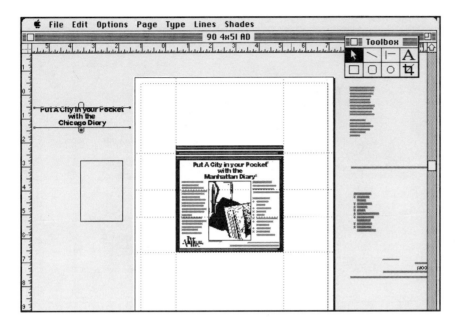

A magazine ad created in PageMaker. The shaded area is the pasteboard where text ands graphics are kept while working on the layout. Shown below PageMaker's image control menu.

Look ma, no T-square

There are two basic types of page-layout programs. PageMaker was designed to work very much like the traditional drawing board where objects needed later are kept off to one side of the page on a pasteboard. Images are sized using the on-screen ruler and by stretching or shrinking them manually using the pointer and the mouse. Though it lacks many fine-tuning features of other programs, PageMaker is a favorite among designers for its free form approach to designing. Quark Xpress and DesignStudio use an "object-oriented" approach to designing pages. Boxes, or special areas, are created on the page. These text and images boxes are placed in the layout using the grid's "snap to" feature. Both programs offer tighter image controls.

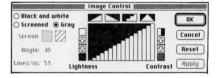

When you start a new design in a page-layout program, a dialog box on the Mac screen asks you to supply some pertinent information about your document. Page size, page orientation (tall or wide), outside margins, and page numbers are all specified from the beginning, but they can be changed later if you wish. Once these parameters are set, your screen displays a blank page. Rulers on the top and left side of the page help you create grids. Columns are easily set up using a dialog box where the number of columns, and the distance between them, is specified. The result of all this is an electronically "ruled" board ready to be converted into a finished layout.

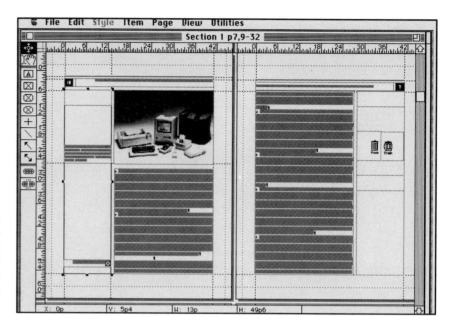

A reduced view of a two-page layout from this book created in Quark-Xpress. Master pages contain headers and page numbers so they don't have to be placed on individual pages. Below is QuarkXpress' image control menu.

For projects like magazines or books that have repetitive page layouts, grids can be set up on "master pages." Creating a master page eliminates having to recreate grids or other repetitious elements like folios on every new page. The master page acts as a template for all these items. If a particular page requires a different grid, the master page option can be turned off for that page.

Image control

Art created in paint and draw programs, as well as scanned art, can be a part of the electronic mechanical. Halftone images can be further lightened or darkened in the page-layout program. In DesignStudio and QuarkXpress, graphics and illustrations can be reduced or enlarged in specific percentages. With PageMaker, image enlargements and reductions are done manually using the mouse and the pointer—you never really know what percentage of the original is achieved. In all three programs, halftones can be adjusted for contrast and line screen.

Working with words

Text can be inserted into a layout by typing it directly onto the page or by "placing" it from a word-processing document. Using the page layout's word processor is handy if you're creating a flyer, letterhead, or other low-text projects. If you have several paragraphs or more of straight text, or are producing a long document like a newsletter, it's better to

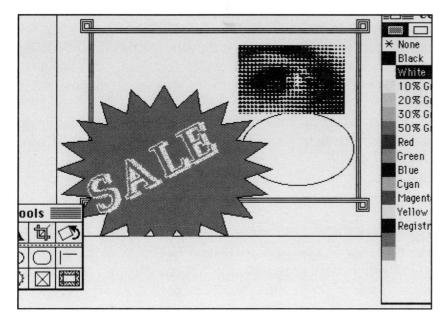

Multi-Ad Creator is a software program that contains special visual tools and features for creating quick advertising layouts.

bring in the copy from a word processor.

Once in the layout, text can be formatted to the designer's needs. This includes: font size; leading within one-half point; tabs and indents; alignment; and tracking and kerning. If you are setting rag text, you can control word breaks. Some programs even let you specify how many broken words appear in any given number of lines. One nice feature for multi-column formats is the "align to baseline" feature that aligns text across columns even if it is broken up by graphics.

If you have repetitive headings and text styles you can elect to create "style sheets." These are dialog boxes that let you define styles for different text elements like body copy, headlines, subheads, etc. Style sheets appear on their own menu. Text is converted to the proper style by highlighting it and choosing the right format from the style sheet menu.

Repasting text after several lines are taken out has been a mechanical artist's nightmare. Page-layout programs make this repositioning unnecessary with an "autoflow" feature that automatically repositions continuous text blocks from column to column on every page. In QuarkXpress and DesignStudio, you can selectively choose how text blocks are linked. In PageMaker the type flows into columns around any graphics in its path.

Running text around artwork has always been a luxury for designers on a tight budget. Sending type back and forth to the typesetter in order to get the wrap just right can be

QuarkXPress®

DesignStudio

PageMaker

expensive. Text wrap options in page-layout programs put an end to this. Every program has its own method for producing text wraps with precision controls. DesignStudio also boasts a feature that makes text conform to geometric shapes like a circle.

All three programs now allow text rotation: PageMaker at 90 degrees, DesignStudio and the new QuarkXpress at any specified angle. DesignStudio and QuarkXpress have the added option of being able to work in a pasteboard mode as well.

Tints, borders, and color

Page design programs have tints and patterns that work much like the ones in drawing programs. In object oriented page-layout programs, borders can be "assigned" to a specific text block. If you're designing a coupon as part of a larger layout, a broken rule border can be assigned to the coupon's text. If the coupon is moved to another part of the layout, the broken rule travels with it. The border will enlarge proportionately if the text area of the coupon is increased.

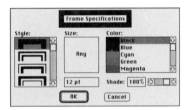

QuarkXpress' frame and line menus.

Borders and rules can be specified in different widths and styles. Scotch rules, broken rules, or dotted lines are all easy to create. The selection in PageMaker is smaller than those offered in QuarkXpress and DesignStudio. Quark has the added luxury of a "frame editor" where the designer can create unique border treatments that can be added to the program's existing border menu.

All three programs offer access to the full range of Pantone colors as well as process colors. This lets you view layouts with color on a color monitor. Remember, as mentioned in the chapter on monitors, screen representations of color are approximate and are affected by countless technological variables. Even if color separations can be produced with PageMaker, DesignStudio, and QuarkXpress, it might be wisest to consider a link to an outside vendor's minicomputer-based system for any true color work (i.e., a professional color separator or retoucher). Chapter 16 discusses the true value of such high-end, pre-press links. Simpler two and three-color jobs are easy to handle with Mac software. Spot colors are produced with effective results in a page-layout program.

Contemplate a template

Designers who work on magazines and in book publishing firms are familiar with preprinted mechanical boards that have the publication's layout grid drawn in nonreproduceable blue lines. That process has advanced many steps further in electronic graphic design through the use of "templates." In many instances, such as a monthly publication or an often used format, a template comes in handy. A template is a page layout document that contains all the information needed to begin designing. Text style sheets, grids, and repetitive artwork are there and ready to use. Templates are created as new documents and saved in a "template" format. Everytime the template is opened it renders an untitled document with all the specifications needed to create the layout. Some software companies manufacture templates for use with their software programs. For designers new to computers, a template can be the springboard into exploring page-layout programs, borrowing a grid from one or style sheets from another. In the design studio, templates can be created for jobs where repetitive layouts and styles are needed.

Designer's checklist: Page layout

■ The page-layout program is where the different elements of the electronic design cycle come together.

■ It is in the higher level of page layout programs where designers will find the specialized features they need. The three major players are PageMaker, QuarkXpress, and DesignStudio.

■ PageMaker uses a traditional drawing board metaphor for its user interface while QuarkXpress and DesignStudio use an object-oriented approach.

■ For projects like magazines or books that have repetitive page layouts, grids can be set up on master pages that eliminate the need to recreate any repetitive elements.

■ Text can be inserted into a layout by typing directly on to the page or by placing text from a word-processing document.

■ Once in the layout, text is formatted according to font, size, leading, tabs, indents, tracking, and kerning.

■ Page layout programs make text repositioning unnecessary with an autoflow feature that automatically repositions continuous text blocks from column to column on every page.

■ All major layout programs offer a full range of color models including Pantone.

Electronic prepress

High resolutions

In the traditional, noncomputerized world of graphic design, type is set by a typesetter and comes back in the form of galleys or repros. In the electronic scenario, entire pages, designed with text and graphics, come out of the Linotronic as repro or camera-ready negatives. Designers who already have experience dealing with typesetters shouldn't have trouble understanding the purpose of a service bureau.

The service bureau has become the high-resolution link in the new electronic graphic design cycle. Service bureaus today provide more than just camera-ready mechanicals. With hardware being so expensive and with technology changing so rapidly, the service bureau steps in to bridge the gap for the design studio. Most service bureaus have scanners, color laser printers, disk converters, and slide makers that transform on-screen designs to finished products. Some offer a range of services that can include photostats and offset printing. Others even have Macintosh rental stations where you can work on a document that might need last minute changes. Since service bureaus figure prominently in the electronic studio, it's a good idea to develop a working relationship with one you can trust.

Quality and cost control The majority of work processed by a service bureau for designers involves Linotronic output. Different firms have

SERVICE OPTIONS (Please Include EPS and TIFF Files; Quark users include Xpress Data and Hyphenation Files)

TURNAROUND	RC PAPER	FILM		COLOR SEPARATIONS
☐ 24Hr. (Standard) ☐ 12hr. (Postscript) ☐ 5hr. (Rush) ☐ Priority	☐ POSTIVE ☐ NEGATIVE	☐ POSITIVE ☐ EMULSION UP ☐ WRONG READING	☐ NEGATIVE ☐ EMULSION DOWN ☐ RIGHT READING	☐ PROCESS (CYMK) ☐ SPOT List Colors

SPECIAL INSTRUCTIONS:

PANTONE® As: (List PMS No.s)
☐ Process (CYMK)
☐ Spot Color

Program/Version	Filename	Crops Y/N	No. of Pages in File	Page No.s to Print or (ALL)	No. of Copies	Total No. of Pages to Rec.	Tall or Wide	Page Size Ltr, Lgl Tab	Screen LPI	DPI 635/1270 /2540

different rates. Some offer good value, others are still new to the business. A bit of homework is essential when choosing the firm that will produce your camera-ready work. It would be encouraging if the process was as simple as taking a disk, putting it in a machine, and watching the latest issue of your newsletter pop out. But it's not.

Poor quality work and unpredictable bills are common if the owner of the service bureau has little or no experience working with designers. Don't be shy about asking for samples of a bureau's previous work. It's also a good idea if you know someone who has used the service. Ask them how their job turned out.

Look at a price list before you start handing out greenbacks. Several factors will determine the cost of printing your document – the resolution or dots per inch (635, 1270, or 2540), the size (up to 11-by-17 inches), the number of pages, and the time it takes to print them. Some services charge only by the page, others also include time charges. On large, complicated jobs it's best to ask for an estimate. Carefully describe the document to be printed, including the number of fonts used and any graphics and halftones that are a part of the design. You might also inquire if the service gives volume discounts.

A little bit of hardware-based questioning is also in order. Does the bureau accept documents by modem? This can be a convenient method of getting high-resolution output if you

A sample service bureau order form for high resolution output. Many service bureaus offer scanning, disk conversions, and slide reproduction as well.

don't live near a service center. One piece of equipment you should know about is Linotronic's newest "raster image processor" (RIP). This device helps print documents faster and hence more inexpensively. The service you use should have the latest version of the RIP installed on their machine.

Be prepared

The most common cause of high-resolution fiascoes is incompatibility. Before taking your disk to a service bureau, make sure that your document is properly prepared. Proofing the pages on a laser printer is one way to spot troublesome errors before you splurge on high resolution. To get clean, crisp, properly formatted copy, the document must be in sync with the device that's printing it. Sending a file for printing that was created using an outdated program will only be a source of headaches. And not using the proper screen fonts will surely send you back to the keyboard.

Font problems are the source of most complications. Be sure your service has the fonts you used in your design. A good bureau will keep a list handy. If you prepare your documents on a Macintosh, don't use the "Style" menu to specify bold, italic, or bold italic type. Always select a specific typeface from your type library (e.g., Bodoni bold or Bodoni italic). Failure to follow this rule will cause character widths to change, which, in turn, affects linebreaks and letterspacing as well.

Documents can take a long time to print if they contain high-density bit-mapped graphics. And if you're paying for output by the minute, your bill will surely skyrocket. Rendering halftone images can also be time-consuming. When you plan your job and execute your document, decide how much you're willing to pay, and be prepared.

Ready to print

So your document is in tip-top shape and you are ready to take the high-resolution leap. Before you release your job to the man behind the counter, there are a few more things to remember. Your disk should be clearly labeled with your name, company, address, and telephone number. Each document should be identified by the name it was given on the disk. The size and resolution of each page along with other information (e.g., fonts used, crop marks, page numbers, application used, etc.) should be written on the job order. The bureau will also want to know if you're printing on film or paper, reverse or positive, and how many copies of each page

Designers working at Macintosh rental stations at Microcomputer Publishing Center in New York City.

are needed. Making sure your bureau has all this information will ensure against difficulties.

Most service bureaus can turn a job around in about 4 to 5 hours. If you're in a hurry, you will pay more. Be careful. As with any design-oriented service, rush charges are expensive.

Quality color reproduction

Many Macintosh programs offer the ability to create color separations from scanned photographs. The question remains unanswered as to whether they can deliver glossy magazine quality. To date, none of these programs has delivered on the promise of design-quality color. Service bureaus are only beginning to address color. Most are not capable of supplying a color key or a chromalin. Nor do they have the expertise to help you color correct them.

Graphic imaging is one of the most complex processes a computer can undertake. That's why a system that costs hundreds of thousands of dollars and requires a trained professional to operate is still the best way to go for stripping and color retouching. The Macintosh wasn't designed for this level of work even though the progress over the years has been remarkable. There is also the question of storing memory-hogging color images. Deficient too, is the level of color scanner available to transfer color image information into the Macintosh.

All this doesn't make the color work created on the

Macintosh a futile effort. A system has evolved whereby Macintosh-generated PostScript files can be transferred into a high-end prepress system for retouching, stripping, and color correction. Companies like Atex Design, Crossfield, CyberChrome, Hell, and Scitex have created their own "prepress links" that yield quality color separations from Macintosh-created work. At this writing, it seems like the best solution for generating professional results. Each company has its own particular software/hardware combination to create the link. Whatever system is chosen, designers should make sure it's compatible with the page-layout software used in their own studios.

Designer's checklist: Electronic prepress

■ Layouts created on a Macintosh are converted to camera ready art using the high resolution imagesetter like a Linotronic. Entire pages with text and graphics in place are output as repro or negatives.

■ Service bureaus are becoming the high resolution link in the new design cycle. Many provide other computer-design services like disk conversion, scanning, and color laser prints.

■ Files prepared for high resolution output must be created with an up-to-date program and have the proper screen fonts. Documents with high density bitmapped images take a long time to print.

■ Four-color separations created using Macintosh technology have not delivered design-quality results as yet.

■ A system has evolved that transfers Mac-generated color files into a high-end, prepress system for retouching, stripping, and color correction

....

Everything in its place

Personal computers proved useful tools for small businesses long before they were used for graphic design. The Macintosh easily handles tasks that include job tracking and scheduling, creating invoices and monthly statements, preparing payroll, and organizing information for income tax returns. Once financial information is in the computer's memory, it's easier to plan and compare numbers from month to month or year to year. Many designers use the computer to maintain mailing lists of existing and potential clients for marketing purposes. With word-processing software, there's even the bonus of good looking business correspondence. In the traditional studio, accounting tasks may be handled by an in-house bookkeeper or an accountant who comes in regularly. In very small studios, the designer/owner may do the books. In either case, moving such information onto the Macintosh is not as difficult as you may think. Once the transition is complete, data is entered and the software program makes all the necessary calculations.

If a design studio already has a computerized accounting system using a non-Mac computer, it may be possible to easily switch or "download" the information directly into the Macintosh. Ask a consultant what would be involved and

The Mac office

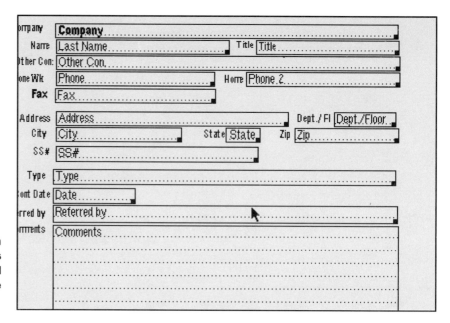

A basic layout for a client file shown in FileMaker. Each field contains information that can be rearranged to suit different tasks. See invoice on next page.

what options you have. Sometimes, all it takes is "linking" software and the proper cable. Many computers use programs that have a Macintosh counterpart, or can read information from your existing files.

The transition need not happen all at once. But you'll be surprised at how quickly you can progress. You can begin by automating invoices, for example, and slowly add those tasks that would be best served by the computer. With the Mac's simple user interface it's easy to learn, and teach others, new software. And just like drawing and page-layout programs, accounting, word-processing, and database programs for the Macintosh let you add a creative touch with rules, typography, and graphics.

There are several ways a design professional can approach computerized filing and record keeping. All of them have merits and, in a sense, can electronically recreate the system you presently use. It's important to assess your requirements and carefully plan before you purchase any office management and accounting software.

I built it myself   A database program is perhaps one of the easiest ways to incorporate a computerized record-keeping system in the design studio. A data base offers a way to create electronic files that are ready to store and calculate information. Most data base software comes with sample templates that can be

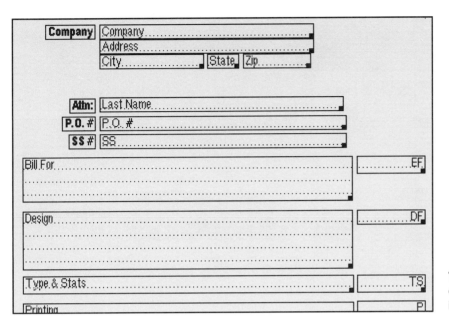

The same FileMaker fields shown on opposite page have been rearranged into an invoice layout.

changed to suit an individual's needs. Building your own data base gives you the advantage of knowing all the elements that went into creating it. There's less of a chance you will get stuck or confused down the road, especially if you keep it simple from the beginning. FileMaker, from Claris Corp., is one of the most popular Macintosh data bases available. Understanding how such programs work gives the designer more office management muscle.

Each entry begins with a "record." Think of a record as an index card where all your client's pertinent information is kept. Data like name, address, telephone, jobs completed, costs, etc., are all entered on the client's record in appropriate "fields." Fields have different purposes. They hold text, numbers, dates, or even art or photos in picture fields. Others store mathematical equations that add, subtract, divide, or otherwise cipher numbers in other fields. Once entered into individual records, fields can be sorted, and information can be rearranged to suit a particular purpose.

"Layouts" use the information in the fields to produce a variety of different documents. A "sort" command lets you find records grouped according to specific fields like name, zip code, or invoice due dates. Form letters, mailing labels, invoices, and monthly billings can all tap on the information in the fields of each client's record. When creating a new layout, the designer selects the fields needed for that

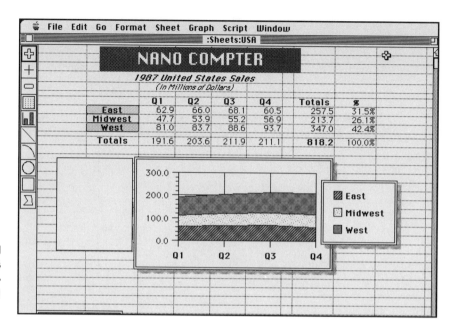

A spreadsheet and chart created using Wingz. Larger design studios can make good use of a spreadsheet/chart program with real number-crunching power.

particular document and positions them on the page, just like in a layout program. You can, for example, create an invoice that draws on the information in a client's individual record. Company name, address, and description of a job are automatically entered while other fields add numbers, give subtotals, calculate sales tax, and produce a final amount due. Aside from invoices, data base programs can help you store information about potential clients as well. You can keep track of direct mail campaigns by using the information in the record to generate follow-up letters. Other popular data base programs include: Microsoft's File, and Panorama from Provue Development Corp.

Designer data   The examples discussed in the previous paragraphs are the products of powerful data base programs. But these are "flat file" data base programs that have limits on how complex and interrelated data can be. There are more powerful "relational" data base programs that require the help of a consultant to create. It takes a trained hand to make sure all the calculations interrelate properly. There are sophisticated job-tracking techniques that can be used by computers on a network so that everyone can enter their respective data on each phase of the project. All of this requires specialized software and a lot of fine tuning. A good consultant will make the transition easier and have you up and running as soon as

```
ESTIMATE  WORKSHEET                    ?  ▦  ◆  ▦

┌──────────┐
│ 3/22/90  │
└──────────┘
PROJECT: Copy of DTP Master Forms        Estimator:

Fees            Rate       Units    General              Rate
Design        $  30 * hr      12    Messengers        $
Art Production                 7    Travel
Photographer                   1    Xerox
Illustrator
Writer                         8
                                    Printing
Production                          Printing           $
Typesetting    $                    Press Check
Linotronic                          Delivery
Photostats
Photoprints
Identicolor
Retouching
```

A sample worksheet from DTP Advisor. There are many Macintosh job-tracking programs designed for ad agencies and designers.

possible. Popular relational data bases include 4th Dimension by Acius, Inc., Double Helix II from Odesta Corporation, FoxBase+ from Fox Software, and Dbase Mac from Ashton-Tate.

Time and expenses

There are several programs for the Macintosh designed for professionals who bill time and expenses. Most of them have features specifically aimed to help ad agencies, graphic designers, and architects. The degree of difficulty of such programs varies. Some come set up for client and time entry information, pretty much ready to use. Software products in this category include: Project Billing by Satori Software, Timeslips III from Timeslips Inc., and Insight Expert Time Billing from Layered, Inc.

Accounting and spreadsheets

In larger design studios, more complex accounting practices may require software that has real number-crunching power. There are several major players in this field. Each of them has a particular attraction. The most popular is Microsoft's Excel. Wingz from Informix Software combines high-powered number crunching with advanced drawing capabilities for designer-quality charts and graphs. Other programs include: Full Impact from Ashton Tate and Trapeze from Access Technology, Inc.

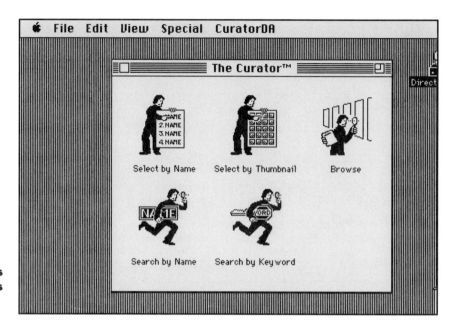

Curator is one of many programs designed to help you index images for easy viewing.

Combined applications

A new breed of office management software that combines the functions of different types of software has recently begun to hit the retail software market. One of these is Microsoft Works, a program that includes spreadsheets, simple drawing tools, a filing system, a word processor, and telecommunications capabilities. This type of program is well-suited for a one-man studio that's just starting out.

Project management

Special project management tools allow you to schedule the various elements of a project, including the costs and dates. When you make changes, the computer updates the information. Included in this type of software are MacProject II from Claris Corporation, MacSchedule from Mainstay, and The DTP Advisor, which includes graphic arts information as well as project management. PrintSpec from StraightEdge Software is a printing specifications program.

Graphic Indexing

There are software programs that help you index images you've created on the Macintosh. These might have been created in drawing or painting programs, through scanning, or computerized clip art. There are several programs that let you create an index or scrapbook in which to store them. These include The Curator, SmartScrap and the Clipper, all from Solutions Incorporated. The Art Importer from Altsys

Corporation turns artwork into keyboard accessible fonts that can be put in a document and handled just as you would a typeface.

Personal scheduling

Time management is easier with a computerized electronic datebook, phone book, or daily planner. Some programs offer the ability to dial phone numbers when the computer is connected to your telephone. Many help you keep track of business leads and contacts. They include: Focal Point from TenPoint0, Colleague from Colleague Business Software Inc., and HyperCard from Apple Computer (supplied free with every Macintosh).

Flexible Forms

If you need to design only an occasional form, consider a page-layout program such as QuarkXpress or DesignStudio for the job. Several dedicated forms programs have been developed for the Mac. Some of these are for designing forms only, while others allow you to fill them in on screen and transfer the information to a data base as well. These include: Smartform Designer and Smartform Assistant from Claris Corp., Fast Forms from Power Up Software, and TrueForm from Adobe Systems.

Designer's checklist: Studio management

■ The Mac can handle many tasks like job tracking and scheduling, invoices, monthly statements, payroll, and organizing information for tax returns.

■ A database program is one easy way to incorporate a computerized record keeping system into the design studio.

■ There are more powerful relational data base programs that require the help of a consultant to create.

■ Other programs for studio management include software for accounting spreadsheets, time and billing , project management image indexing, personal scheduling, or creating forms.

Multimedia and beyond

18 Design for a paperless society

The graphic designer of the future will be nursed on video games and use a computer long before the first year of art school. Design in the future will move beyond creating pages that are printed on paper. With more and more personal computers in the home and office, it won't be long before monitors and television sets assume the role of electronic newspapers, books, and magazines.

Tomorrow's designer will be called upon to create layouts that look good on a monitor as well as on paper. It's already starting to happen. Last year, Domino Pizza's corporate office commissioned a version of their annual report on a floppy disk for viewing on a personal computer. *MacWeek* uses a HyperCard stack with animated type and graphics as an advertising media kit. Software retailers point to a new market for books on laser disk that are viewed on a personal computer. Interactive technologies, animation, 35mm slides, video, and digitized sound will all be a part of the toolbox of the future. These new techniques are available today in varying stages of development. In five years, most will be perfected. Designing for print and paper won't end but it will have to compete with many more mediums. Apple is calling the new technology desktop media.

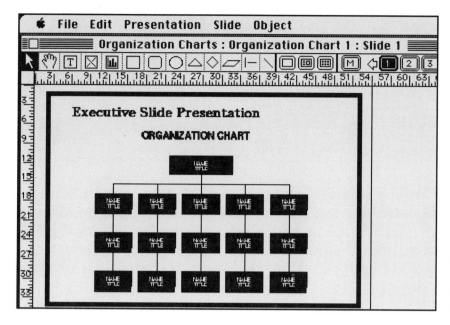

Standout is a Macintosh program dedicated to designing and producing color slides. Slide-making programs offer a variety of color backgrounds, simple drawing tools, and text capabilities.

The process of preparing color slides and overhead transparencies for presentation used to be handled by slide service bureaus. Working under the designer's supervision, 35mm slides with text and graphics would be created in full color. Today, these same bureaus advertise that they'll take your Macintosh files and convert them into slides with all of the design intact.

There are several Macintosh programs dedicated to designing and producing color slides. They offer a variety color backgrounds, simple drawing tools, and text capabilities. Many offer a feature that lets you edit the sequence of the slides and view them on your monitor as a complete presentation. Slides can be processed with a film recorder (see Chapter 8) or by sending them to a service bureau.

Programs for creating slides on the Macintosh include Aldus' Persuasion, CA Cricket Presents from Computer Associates, PowerPoint by Microsoft Corporation, and Standout from Letraset. All of these range in price from $300 - $400. One interesting package for producing slides is More II by Symantec Corp. This program combines an electronic outliner where ideas are organized, then converted into bullets or flow charts prior to placing them into an on-screen or slide presentation.

Before you send your slides out for processing, make sure that the bureau accepts files from the program you used.

Kill the lights, please

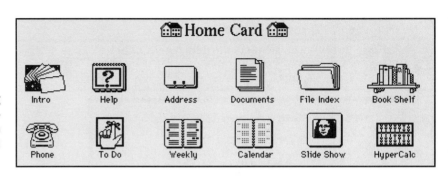

Hypercard stacks are created using HyperTalk, a simple computer language that uses plain English. Each card can hold text, graphics, digitized sounds and animation.

Text, type, and information graphics

Creating charts and graphs for presentations and reports, on or off-screen, is a natural for the Macintosh. If drawn with chart and graph software, values on a chart can be changed and those changes are instantly redrawn. Information is quickly updated. All of the latest Macintosh spreadsheet programs offer chart-making capabilities. (See Chapter 17) Colors, rules, text, type, and choice of chart are user definable.

Multimedia

Using slides in a presentation is a tried and true form of communicating with a room full of people. But now, many companies are using the Mac to generate graphics and text in an interactive environment, completely changing how presentations are assembled and viewed. It is now possible to connect your Macintosh to many audio and visual sources, from video recorders to electronic pianos. And the tool being used to organize and combine all of these elements is Apple's HyperCard, a software program distributed free with the Macintosh since 1986.

HyperCard

To understand hypercard, imagine a stack of multimedia index cards. With HyperCard you create a "stack" of such cards. Stacks are assembled with "scripts" created in HyperTalk, a simple computer language written in plain English. Each card can hold text, graphics, digitized sounds, and animation. You flip through the stack much like you would a stack of index cards. Special "buttons" on each card direct you to sub-stacks that can give further information about a particular topic. Buttons can also activate sounds and animated images. HyperCard allows a complex subject to be initially presented in a simple format with more detailed information accessible at the viewer's discretion. It can't be beat as a front-end tool for multimedia presentations. Another popular multimedia software package is MacroMind Director which creates

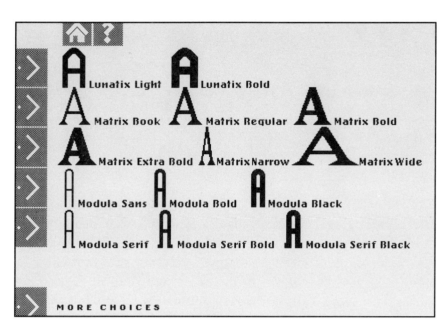

Samples of Emigre typefaces, designed by Zuzana Licko, are placed into a HyperCard stack for quick and easy viewing. Potential type buyers can see the styles on their Macintoshes before they purchase fonts.

animations on the Macintosh screen. These can be a simple moving images, or complex, animated forms and shapes. Super 3D from Silicon Beach Software draws three dimensional images, then rotates and moves them so you can create simple animated effects.

On the horizon

Let's hope that a beautifully printed book, with its just-off-the-press feel and smell, never becomes extinct. But, who knows? Technology has changed the way information is being presented. Computerized, interactive shows appeal to public sensibilities that are fed on sound bites and rapidly changing video images. The challenge for the graphic designer of tomorrow will be to communicate through the din and to stay abreast of technological advancements. The sooner you learn about the new technology, the sooner you can be a part of it.

Designer's checklist: Multimedia and beyond

■ Tomorrow's graphic designer will create layouts that look good on a monitor as well as on paper.

■Interactive technologies, animation, 35mm slides, video, and digitized sound will all be a part of the toolbox of the future.

■There are a variety of Macintosh programs dedicated to designing and producing color slides.

■ It is now possible to connect a Macintosh to many audio and visual sources, from video recorders to electric pianos and assemble the input into multimedia presentations.

■ HyperCard, a multimedia application from Apple, allows a complex subject to be presented in a simple format with more detailed information accessible at the viewer's discretion.

Appendices

PART IV

Suggested Reading

Periodicals

**Computer Buyer's Guide
and Handbook**
P.O. Box 318
Mt. Morris, IL 61054
(800) 435-0715

Desktop Communications
P.O. Box 94175
Atlanta, GA 30341
(800) 966-9052

MacUser
P.O. Box 56986
Boulder, CO 80321
(800) 525-0643

MacWEEK
P.O. Box 5821
Cherry Hill, NJ 08034
(609) 428-5000

Macworld
Subscriber Services
P.O. Box 54529
Boulder, CO 80322-4529
(800) 525-0643
(303) 447-9330

Personal Publishing
Hitchcock Publishing Company
191 S. Gary Avenue
Carol Stream, IL 60188
(708) 665-1000

Publish!
Subscriber Services
P.O. Box 55400
Boulder, CO 80322
(800) 274-5116

Books

**Graphic Design for the
Electronic Age**
by Jan V. White, 1988,
Watson-Guptil Publications

**Design & Technology,
Erasing the Boundaries**
by Wendy Richmond, 1990,
Van Nostrand Reinhold

The Macintosh Font Book
by Erfert Fenton, 1989,
Peachpit Press

The Macintosh Bible
edited by Arthur Naiman, 1989,
Goldstein & Blair

The Big Mac Book
by Neil J. Salkind, 1989,
Que Corporation

**The Language of Computer
Publishing**
by Dr. Donald J. Brenner, 1990,
Brenner Information Group

**Getting Started in
Computer Graphics**
by Gary Olsen, 1990,
North Light Books

Encyclopedia Macintosh
by Craig Danuloff and Deke
McClelland, 1990,
Sybex

Glossary

active window The front most window displayed on the Macintosh screen. An active window's title bar is highlighted.

anti-aliasing The process by which the appearance of jagged lines that result from the limited resolution of a graphic display are smoothed. Software and programs correct the stepped appearance of diagonal and curved lines by averaging intensities between neighboring pixels to soften the staircase effect.

AppleTalk A local area network, built into all Macintoshes, which allow the computer to share files and peripherals, such as printers. AppleTalk can be installed into other computers.

application program Software used to manipulate information, sometimes referred to simply as an "application."

ASCII American [National] Standard Code for Information Interchange. A generic code for representing alpha-numeric characters, allowing for the exchange of information between different operating systems.

autoflow A setting found in many page-layout programs that allows for continuous placement of blocked text from page to page without operator intervention.

autotrace A mode found in some drawing programs that creates a set of vectors to represent outlines on a bitmapped image. This is used to capture hand drawings in computer-aided design and to create draw-style images from paint-style images.

baud The unit of measurement for the speed at which a modem transmits information over a telephone wire.

Bezier curve A curve often used in drawing programs. It is defined by specifying control points that set the shape of the curve.

bitmap A set of pixels, or picture elements, that represent a graphic image or a font.

bus A set of connectors on the back of a Macintosh that are used to attach the keyboard, mouse, and other devices such as digitized tablets, hand controls, and specialized keyboards.

central processing unit (CPU) The main manipulatory section of a computer, which contains the arithmetic-logical unit and registers.

chip A small integrated circuit package containing thousands of logic elements. An "8K" device contains 8,000 circuits.

click To position the pointer on something, then quickly press and release the mouse button.

clipboard A feature on the Macintosh that temporarily holds the information last cut or copied; a buffer area in the memory.

clipping path An outline, in a graphics program, which is used to select a portion of an object to be manipulated.

close box The small white box on the far left side of an active window's title bar. Clicking the close box closes the window.

color resolution The number of different colors or gray-scale values a system can produce or work with. A value is usually given in bits.

command A code that can be key-boarded and entered in a computer's memory that will instruct the typesetter or other device concerning the handling and disposition of the text or graphics. Often, codes used in typesetting are combinations of characters that form abbreviations for command names.

connector point A point, in certain drawing programs, where a curve meets a line segment with the end of the curve colinear with the line. It marks a smooth transition from curve to line.

control panel A desk accessory used to personalize the Macintosh's different features. The control panel is used to adjust the speaker volume, set the clock, and access other control panel devices.

control points Points that determine the shape of the curve, but that do not necessarily lie along the path of the curve. The shape of bezier curves are determined in this matter.

cursor A movable symbol, usually blinking, that appears on the screen of a terminal and can be positioned vertically and horizontally to indicate at which point an action is to be taken.

cut and paste The equivalent of using scissors to clip something and glue or paste it somewhere else. Moving data from one place in a document to another place or to another document.

desk accessory (DA) Utilities available on the Apple menu regardless of which application is presently in use. Mini-applications such as the Alarm Clock, Scrapbook, Key Caps, the Control Panel, and the Calculator are installed by using the Font/DA Mover.

desktop The Macintosh computer's on-screen working environment – the menu bar and the gray area on the screen.

dialog box An on-screen box that contains a message requesting more information from the Macintosh user. Sometimes the message is a warning that the user is about to destroy information or has given an unexecutable command.

digitized type Type stored in computer readable form as a collection of dots or line elements.

digitizer A computer peripheral device that converts an analog signal (images or sound) into a digital signal. With an image, the digitizer sends position information to the computer, either on a command from the user or at regular intervals. Digitizers are available in various sizes, ranging from tabletop models to large stand-alone units.

disk drive The system or device that electromagnetically reads information from or writes information on a magnetic storage disk.

dithering A means of simulating gray levels on a laser printer or computer screen that cannot print gray-scale halftone dots. Dithering varies the shape of the dots themselves; the eye reads the dithered area as a gray value.

document Anything created using Macintosh software.

Glossary

dot-matrix printer A low-resolution printer that forms letters and images using a matrix of dots.

dots per inch A measure of printer resolution or density. The dpi determines the overall appearance or quality of the printed output. Laser text is often 300 dpi.

double-click A technique used in selecting and opening files. The pointer is used to select, then the mouse button is pressed and released twice in quick succession without moving the mouse.

downloadable font A font is downloaded into a printer when tables telling how to construct characters are sent from the computer to the output device. A printer must have sufficent memory and processing power to receive and store these images.

drag A technique used for choosing commands, moving elements on screen, and selecting text.

embedded command With reference to output-formatting commands in a word-processing system, these commands for the printer are included within the regular text, rather than specified in a separate file by keyboard commands.

encapsulated PostScript (EPS) A graphic file format that includes one representation of the image in PostScript and a preview representation of the picture in a PICT format that is used to draw it on the screen. EPS files usually print sharp images but occupy a good deal of disk space.

expansion card A circuit board that plugs into a computer and gives it additional specialized functions.

expansion slots Slots in a computer into which you insert expansion cards.

export The output of text, graphics, or layouts from a program in a form suitable for use with other programs.

firmware Software in a hardware form such as on a chip.

flatbed scanner A flatbed scanner is similar to a photocopier in that original art to be scanned is positioned face down on a glass plate. Its design accommodates books. Its exact alignment of the original page produces more precise results than sheet-fed scanners that feed the image into the scanner with rollers.

floppy disk A thin, flexible circular film with a magnetic surface capable of storing digitized information, enclosed in a thin, plastic case. A 3 1/2-inch floppy disk is used on a Macintosh.

font A complete assortment or set of all the characters of a particular typeface, all of one size and style.

font style A set of stylistic variations, such as bold, outline, underline, and italic.

Font/DA Mover An application by which fonts and desk accessories may be added or removed from a Macintosh computer disk's system file or desk accessory file.

frame A unit of design, in some desktop-publishing programs, which can contain text, graphics, or both. A series of frames can make up a page.

graphics program A tool that produces drawings, designs, charts, and manipulates images on the computer.

gray scale Representation of images using different levels of gray tone. Halftone images employ gray scale by varying the density of the halftone dots. Shades of gray on the screen that are created by varying the intensity of the screen's pixels, rather than by using a combination of black and white pixels to produce shading. Black and white televisions are gray scale. Most computer screens are not.

hard disk A disk drive with a permanently encased storage disk. Hard disks usually boast high-volume storage capacities and can be housed inside a computer or in an external case.

hardware The actual equipment that makes up a computer system.

hierarchical file system A feature that allows you to use folders to organize documents, applications, and other folders on a disk. Folders can be put within other folders to create as many levels as needed.

highlight Selecting or choosing an element and making it distinct from its background. In a word-processing program, for example, words are highlighted if they are going to be erased or changed.

icon The unique graphic image used on the Macintosh desktop to represent a particular software application, a file, a concept, or a message.

input The raw data, text, or commands inserted into a computer.

input devices Light pens, keyboards, graphic tablets, touch sensitive screens, or any device used to give a computer information.

interactive Immediate response to input. In interactive processing, an image can be modified or edited and the changes can be seen right away.

interface A common boundary between systems or parts of systems. Usually some form of an electronic device that enables one computer system to accept the protocols of another in such a way that data or programs designated for one system are useable on the other.

jaggies The jagged, stair-like lines that appear in both type characters and graphics when the computer screen or printer fails to convert digital data into a smooth image.

landscape monitor A video display screen whose width is greater then its height, like a pastoral landscape painting.

local area network Linking multiple computers so that they may share files and peripherals such as printers.

marquee A rectangular area surrounded by blinking dashes or dotted lines, used to select objects or regions in a drawing program.

megabyte (Mb) A unit of measurement equal to 1024 kilobytes. It is commonly used in specifying the capacity of computer memory.

memory The area in a computer into which data can be entered and stored for later retrieval.

menu A list of choices presented by a particular program, by which a desired action may be selected. In the desktop interface, menus appear when you point to and click on menu titles on the menu bar. To select a certain command, drag through the menu and release the mouse button while a command is highlighted.

Glossary

menu bar A horizontal strip at the top of the screen that contains menu titles.

microcomputer A small computer containing a microprocessor, input and display devices, and memory all in one box. Usually known as a personal computer or desktop computer.

microprocessor A single chip or integrated circuit containing the entire central processing unit.

mode A device that links one computer to other computers and information services through telephone lines.

monitor A video display terminal that serves as the user's window on the computer's doings.

monofont A font in which each character occupies the same horizontal width as any other; also referred to as a monospaced font or fixed-pitch font.

mouse A small box-like device that is moved around on a flat surface next to the computer. Its position and motion controls the on-screen cursor to select operations, to move data, and to draw.

MultiFinder A first-generation multi-tasking operating system for Macintosh computers that makes it possible to have several applications open at the same time. It also allows you to perform applications such as printing in the background, while retaining use of your computer for other applications in the foreground.

multimedia Any audiovisual presentation that uses more than one medium such as slides, video, sound, and film.

object-oriented In computer-aided drawing, an approach to maintaining individual elements and groups of elements as objects for ease of manipulation and revision. In drawing and layout programs, an approach that treats graphics as line and arc segments rather than individual dots.

on-line Equipment that is in direct communication with the central processor of a computer system, as opposed to offline devices.

optical character recognition (OCR) An electronic way to scan printed or written information and translate the scanned image into a computer text file.

page-description language A computer language that describes how text and graphics should be placed on a page for display or printing. Any output is generated by computer programs and read by printers, without direct human intervention.

page preview A mode found on many word-processing programs and page-layout programs that shows a full-page view of how a page will look when printed out, including added elements such as headers, footers, and margins.

paste Placing a copy of saved material into a document or layout.

path A combination of lines, points, and curves that can be drawn into one operation in a drawing program.

peripheral equipment The input / output units and secondary storage units of a computer system. The central processor and its associated storage and control units are the only parts of a computer system which are not considered peripheral equipment.

PICT A format for storage and exchange of graphics documents on the Macintosh and the format used by the clipboard.

PICT 2 An update of the basic Apple format for the storage and exchange of graphics documents on the Macintosh. PICT2 adds support for color and for more formatting instructions carried as comments within the image file.

pixel The picture element is the smallest visual unit on the screen that can be stored, displayed, or modified. It is also a location in video memory that corresponds to a point on the graphics screen when the viewing window includes that location. Images that are created with pixels are referred to as bitmapped.

pointer A small arrow on the screen that follows the movement of the mouse.

pointer tool A tool used in layout and drawing programs to select objects or an entire block of text. It is usually represented by an on-screen arrow.

pointing device An input device such as a mouse used to indicate where an on-screen pointer should be placed or moved.

port A connection between a computer and other units such as peripherals or networks. Ports are often known by the type of signals they carry, such as a printer port or a serial port.

portrait monitor A video display screen whose height is greater than its width, like a portrait painting.

posterize To transform an image to a more stark version by rounding tonal values.

PostScript Adobe Systems' page description language. PostScript is built into a printer if it includes a processor that runs a program that translates statements in the PostScript language to the corresponding marks made by the printer. A software program is considered PostScript compatible if it translates statements in the PostScript page-description language.

print area The area on which an output device can place a mark, most often expressed within the bounds of a rectangle. On most electronic and image-processing devices, this is smaller than the full sheet of paper resulting in an area that is smaller than the page size.

print spooler A utility that writes a representation of a document's printed image to disk or to memory, schedules it to print in a que of other jobs, and then prints it. The spooler frees up the computer while printing is in process.

printer A device that receives information and instructions from your computer and produces images of text and graphics on paper.

printer font A font that a printer uses.

QuickDraw Built-in drawing routines that perform all graphics operations on the Macintosh. It is the foundation of most Macintosh graphics programs.

radial fill A varying color or tint that changes smoothly from one color or brightness to another, usually moving from the center of an object out toward the edges.

random access memory (RAM) Data storage in which records or individual bytes are accessible independent of their location in relation to the previous record or byte accessed.

raster image file format (RIFF) A file format for paint-style graphics.

Glossary

read only memory (ROM) Stores permanent information used repeatedly, such as computer control functions or characters for electronic display.

refresh rate The rate at which a monitor display is regenerated.

resolution The number of pixels per unit of area. The sharpness of an image on a screen or in printed form, measured in dots, spots, or lines per inch.

RGB A method of displaying a color video signal by transmitting primary colors as separate signals. In RGB, color is defined as percentages of red, green, and blue.

saturation A subjective term that refers to the difference of a hue from a gray of the same value. In a subtractive system, adding the complement makes the color darker. In an additive system, adding the complement will make the color lighter.

scan To convert an image from visible form to an electronic description.

scanner An input device that converts printed matter into bit data so it can be read, stored, and manipulated electronically by the computer.

screen fonts A set of characters designed for display on a computer monitor and adapted for its resolution.

scroll bar Clicking or dragging in the scroll bar allows you to move through the document.

small computer systems interface (SCSI) An interface between computers and peripheral device controllers used by the Macintosh. It provides high-speed access to peripheral devices. In computer circles, pronounced "scuzzy."

snap, snap to The automatic movement of a selected object or point to the nearest designated grid line, grid intersection, or connection point.

software A program or collection of programs that control the computer.

startup disk A disk that has all the necessary program and system files contained in the system folder for the Macintosh to set the computer in operation. Often called a boot disk.

stroke Making a defined path part of an image by giving it visible characteristics such as line or color in a drawing program or page-description language.

style Variation in the appearance of a typeface, for example italic, underlined, outlined, or shadow.

style sheets In word-processing and page-layout programs, formatting instructions that can be applied to individual files.

system An integrated assembly of hardware and software designed to run a given application or set of applications.

system software Special files on the Macintosh that contain the operating system program and its supporting and auxillary programs.

tag image file format (TIFF) A graphic file format developed by Apple, Aldus, and Adobe for gray-scale data. It is suited for representing scanned images and other large bitmaps. Newer versions of TIFF support color and compression.

tape backup A mechanism that reads and writes information on magnetic tape.

telecommunications Communication from one computer terminal or system to another via telephone lines.

tile A single sheet or portion that can be combined with others to form an oversize page, or to split a page into such sections.

tool An object or icon used to perform operations in a computer program. Tools are often named either by what they do or by the type of object on which they work.

utility programs Support programs such as editors, assemblers, and anti-virus packages.

value Comparison of a chromatic color to an achromatic color along the gray scale from white to black. Synonyms are: intensity, brilliance, or brightness.

window The area on the Macintosh desktop screen that displays information. Documents are viewed through a window. A window can be opened or closed, or moved around the desktop.

word processor A system or program that allows for the writing, editing, correcting, arranging, storing, and printing of a display of text.

work station Configuration of computer equipment designed to be used by one person at a time. A work station may have a terminal connected to a larger computer or may "stand alone" with local processing capability.

WYSIWYG What you see is what you get—what you see on the screen is an accurate image of what you will see printed out. In computer circles, pronounced "wiz-ee-wig."

zoom box The box on the right side of the title bar on some windows. When the zoom box is clicked, the window expands to its maximum size. Clicking it again returns the window to its original size.

Vendors

Apple Computer, Inc.
20525 Mariani Avenue
Cupertino, CA 95014
(408) 996-1010
*Complete line of computers
and peripherals.*

Monitors

Cornerstone Technology
1883 Ringwood Avenue
San Jose, CA 95131
(408) 279-1600

E-Machines, Inc.
9305 S.W. Gemini Drive
Beaverton, OR 97005
(503) 646-6699

MegaGraphics, Inc.
439 Calle San Pablo
Camarillo, CA 93012
(805) 484-3799

Nutmeg Systems Inc.
25 South Avenue
New Canaan, CT 06840
(203) 966-3226

**Personal Computer
Peripherals Corp.**
4710 Eisenhower Blvd.
Tampa, FL 33634
(800) 622-2888

Radius Inc.
1710 Fortune Drive St.
San Jose, CA 95131
(408) 434-1010

RasterOps Corporation
10161 Bubb Road
Cupertino, CA 95014
(408) 446-4090

Sigma Designs Inc.
46501 Landing Parkway
Fremont, CA 94538
(415) 770-0100

SuperMac Technology
485 Potrero Avenue
Sunnyvale, CA 94086
(408) 773-4470

Input

Calcomp
2411 West LaPalma Avenue
Anaheim, CA 92801
(800) 225-2667
WIZ -mouse/tablet

Datadesk International
7651 Haskell Avenue
Van Nuys, CA 91406
(800) 826-5398
Mac 101 enhanced keyboard

Hewlett-Packard Co.
19310 Pruneridge Avenue
Cupertino, CA 95104
(800) 752-0900
HP ScanJet scanner

Kensington Microware, Ltd.
251 Park Avenue South
New York, NY 10010
(800) 535-4242
ADB Turbo MousePlus

Logitech, Inc.
6505 Kaiser Drive
Fremont, CA 94555
(415) 795-8500
Hand scanners

Sharp Electronics Corp.
Sharp Plaza Box C
Mahwah, NJ 07430
(201) 529-9500
Color scanners

Summagraphics Corp.
60 Silvermine Road
Seymour, CT 06483
(203) 881-5400
Graphics tablets

Thunderware Inc.
21 Orinda Way
Orinda, CA 94563
(415) 254-6581
scanners

Wacom, Inc.
139 West 115 Century Road
Paramus, NJ 07652
(201) 265-4722
Graphics tablets

Output

Advanced Matrix Tech.
100 Rancho Road
Thousand Oaks, CA 91361
(800) 637-7898
MacDot-Color dot matrix

AGFA Matrix
1 Ramland Road
Orangeburg, NY 10962
(800) 852-8533
Film recorders

Dataproducts Corp.
6200 Canoga Avenue
Woodland Hills, CA 91365
(818) 887-8000
Laser printers

GCC Technologies, Inc.
580 Winter Street
Waltham, MA 02154
(617) 890-0880
Laser & ink jet printers

Mirus Corporation
4301 Great America Pkwy.
Santa Clara, CA 95054
(800) 654-0808
Slide makers

Mitsubishi Electronics, Inc.
991 Knox Street
Torrance, CA 90502
(213) 515-3993
Color thermal printers

Presentation Technologies
743 N. Pastoria Avenue
Sunnyvale, CA 94086
(408) 749-1959
Slide makers

QMS Inc.
One Magnum Pass
Mobile, AL 36618
(800) 631-2693
Laser printers

Qume Corp.
500 Yosemite Drive
Milpitas, CA 95035
(408) 942-4000
Laser printers

Storage / Backup

Central Point Software, Inc.
15220 NW Greenbrier Pkwy.
Beaverton, OR 97006
(503) 690-8090
PC Tools/Mac-disk utilities

Ehman Inc.
P. O. Box 2126
Evanston, WY 82931
(800) 257-1666
storage device

Fifth Generation Systems
11200 Industrialplex Blvd.
Baton Rouge, LA 70809
(800) 873-4384
Fastback Mac

GCC Technologies, Inc.
580 Winter Street
Waltham, MA 02154
(617) 890-0880
Storage devices

Iomega Corporation
1821 West 4000
South Roy, UT 84067
(801) 778-3000
Bernoulli removable storage

La Cie, Ltd.
16285 SW 85th Street #306
Tigard, OR 97224
(503) 684-0143
Storage devices

Mirror Technologies, Inc.
2644 Patton Road
Roseville, MN 55113
(800) 654-5294
Storage devices

Rodime Systems
851 Broken Sound Pkwy. NW
Boca Raton, FL 33487
(407) 994-5585
Storage devices

Symantec Corporation
10201 Torre Avenue
Cupertino, CA 95104
(800) 441-7234
SUM-hard disk utilities

Vendors

Utilities

Alsoft, Inc.
P.O. Box 927
Spring, TX 77383
(713) 353-4090
MasterJuggler-font mgmt.

Altsys Corp.
720 Avenue F
Plano, TX 75074
(214) 424-4888
*Art Importer, Metamorposis,
Fontastic Plus, Fontagrapher*

Berkeley Systems, Inc.
1700 Shattuck Avenue
Berkeley, CA 94709
(415) 540-5536
Stepping Out-screen extender

CE Software
1854 Fuller Road
West Des Moines, IA 50265
(515) 224-1995
DiskTop-desktop manager

Fifth Generation Systems
1322 Bell Avenue
Tustin, CA 92680
(800) 873-4384
Suitcase-font mgmt.

HJC Software, Inc.
P.O. Box 51816
Durham, NC 27717
(919) 490-1277
Virex-virus protection

Mainstay
5311-B Derry Avenue
Agoura Hills, CA 91301
(818) 991-6540
Capture-screen capture

Sabastian Software
P.O. Box 70278
Bellevue, WA 98007
(206) 861-0602
Image Grabber

Solutions International
30 Commerce Street
Williston, VT 05495
(802) 658-5506
*The Curator,
SmartScrap & The Clipper*

Word processing

Ashton-Tate
20101 Hamilton Avenue
Torrance CA, 90502
(213) 329-8000
FullWrite Professional

Claris Corporation
5201 Patrick Henry Drive
Santa Clara, CA 95052
(800) 334-3535
MacWrite II

DeltaPoint, Inc.
200 Heritage Harbor
Monterey, CA 93940
(800) 367-4334
MindWrite

Deneba Software
3305 N.W. 74th Avenue
Miami, FL 33122
(800) 622-6287
Big Thesaurus

Microsoft Corp.
16011 N.E. 36th Way
Redmond, WA 98073
(800) 426-9400
*Microsoft Word
MicrosoftWrite*

Paragon Concepts, Inc.
990 Highland Drive
Solana Beach, CA 92075
(619) 481-1477
Nisus

Symmetry Corp.
761 E. University Drive
Mesa, AZ 85203
(800) 624-2485
Acta Advantage-outliner

T/Maker Co.
1390 Villa Street
Mountain View, CA 94041
(415) 962-0195
WriteNow

WordPerfect Corporation
1555 N. Technology Way
Orem, UT 84057
(801) 225-5000
WordPerfect

Drawing

Adobe Systems Inc.
1585 Charleston Road
Mountain View, CA 94039
(415) 961-4400
*Adobe Illustrator 88
Streamline-tracing software*

Aldus Corporation
411 First Avenue S.
Seattle, WA 98104
(206) 622-5500
Aldus FreeHand

Broderbund Software, Inc.
17 Paul Drive
San Rafael, CA 94903
(800) 521-6262
Drawing Table

Claris Corporation
5201 Patrick Henry Drive
Santa Clara, CA 95052
(800) 334-3535
MacDraw II

Computer Associates
601 Gateway Boulevard S.
San Francisco, CA 94080
(415) 875-1600
CA-Cricket Draw

Deneba Software
3305 N.W. 74th Avenue
Miami, FL 33122
(800) 622-6287
Canvas

Micromaps
PO Box 757
Lambertville, NJ 08530
(800) 334-4291
Mapping software

Software for Recognition
55 Academy Drive
Rochester, NY 14623
(716) 359-3024
MiniDraw

Zedcor, Inc.
4500 East Speedway
Tucson, AZ 85712
(800) 482-4567
DeskPaint and DeskDraw

Painting

Claris Corporation
5201 Patrick Henry Drive
Santa Clara, CA 95052
(800) 334-3535
MacPaint

Computer Friends, Inc.
14250 NW Science Park Dr.
Portland, OR 97229
(503) 626-2291
Modern Artist

Deneba Software
3305 N.W. 74th Avenue
Miami, FL 33122
(800) 622-6287
UltraPaint

Electronic Arts
1820 Gateway Drive
San Mateo, CA 94404
(800) 245-4525
Studio/1, Studio/8

LaserWare Inc.
PO Box 668
San Rafael, CA 94915
(800) 367-6898
LaserPaint Color II

MicroIllusions
17408 Chatsworth Street
Granada Hills, CA 91344
((800) 522-2041
Photon Paint

NuEquation, Inc.
1701 N. Greenville Avenue
Richardson, TX 75801
(214) 699-7747
NuPaint

Qualitas Trading Co.
6907 Norfolk Road
Berkeley, CA 94705
(415) 848-8080
MacCalligraphy

Silicon Beach Software
9770 Carroll Center Road
San Diego, CA 92126
(619) 695-6956
SuperPaint

Vendors

Image processing

Avalon Development Group
1000 Massachusetts Ave.
Cambridge, MA 02138
(800) 522-0265
PhotoMac

Letraset USA
40 Eisenhower Drive
Paramus, NJ 07653
(800) 526-9073
ColorStudio, ImageStudio

Silicon Beach Software
9770 Carroll Center Road
San Diego, CA 92126
(619) 695-6956
Digital Darkroom

SuperMac Technology
485 Potrero Avenue
Sunnyvale, CA 94086
(408) 773-4470
PixelPaint Professional

Type

Adobe Systems Inc.
1585 Charleston Road
Mountain View, CA 94039
(415) 961-4400
Adobe typeface library
Adobe Type Manager
Adobe Type Reunion
Smart Art Effects I, II, III

Agfa Compugraphic
90 Industrial Way
Wilmington, MA 01887
(800) 622-8973
CG Type for the Macintosh

Altsys Corp.
720 Avenue F
Plano, TX 75074
(214) 424-4888
Fontographer, Fontastic plus
Metamorphosis-converts
fonts to outlines

Bitstream
215 First Street
Cambridge, MA 02142
(617) 497-6222
Bitstream typeface library

Broderbund Software, Inc.
17 Paul Drive
San Rafael, CA 94903
(800) 521-6262
TypeStyler

Casady & Greene
P.O. Box 223779
Carmel, CA 93922
(408) 624-8716
Fluent Laser Fonts

EDCO Services, Inc.
12410 N. Dale Mabry Hwy.
Tampa, FL 33618
(813) 962-7800
LetrTuck Plus-kerning

Icom Simulations, Inc.
648 S. Wheeling Road
Wheeling, IL 60090
(312) 520-4440
MacKern-kerning

Image Club Graphics Inc.
1902 11th Street SE
Calgary, Alberta, Canada
(800) 661-9410
LetterPress CD ROM fonts

Kingsley/ATF
2559-2 E. Broadway
Tucson, AZ 85716
(602) 325-5884
ATF Classic Type fonts
ATF Type Designer

Letraset USA
40 Eisenhower Drive
Paramus, NJ 07653
(800) 526-9073
LetraStudio, LetraFont
Library, FontStudio

Linotype Co.
425 Oser Avenue
Hauppauge, NY 11788
(800) 426-7705
Linotype's font library

Postcraft International
27811 Avenue Hopkins
Valencia, CA 91355
(805) 257-1797
Laser FX-font enhancer

Page layout

Aldus Corporation
411 First Avenue S.
Seattle, WA 98104
(206) 622-5500
PageMaker

Interleaf, Inc
10 Canal Park
Cambridge, MA 02141
(617) 577-9800
Interleaf Publisher

Letraset USA
40 Eisenhower Drive
Paramus, NJ 07653
(800) 526-9073
DesignStudio, ReadySetGo!

Lightspeed Computer Co.
47 Farnsworth Street
Boston, MA 02210
(617) 338-2173
LightSpeed

Quark, Inc.
300 South Jackson Street
Denver, CO 80209
(800) 356-9363
QuarkXPress, QuarkStyle

Ragtime USA
400 Walnut Street
Redwood City, CA 94063
(415) 780-1800
Ragtime-integrated page
Processing

Silicon Beach Software
9770 Carroll Center Road
San Diego, CA 92126
(619) 695-6956
PersonalPress

SpringBoard Software, Inc.
7808 Creekridge Circle
Minneapolis, MN 55435
(800) 445-4780
SpringBoard Publisher

Timeworks, Inc.
444 Lake Cook Road
Deerfield, IL 60015
(312) 948-9200
Publish It!

Prepress

Agfa Compugraphic
90 Industrial Way
Wilmington, MA 01887
(800) 622-8973
Laser printers / imagesetters

Aldus Corporation
411 First Avenue S.
Seattle, WA 98104
(206) 622-5500
Aldus Preprint

Linotype Co.
425 Oser Avenue
Hauppauge, NY 11788
(800) 426-7705
Imagesetters

Scitex America Corp.
8 Oak Park Drive
Bedford, MA 01730
(617) 275-5150
Visionary-color

Varityper Inc.
11 Mount
Pleasant Avenue
East Hanover, NJ 07936
(800) 631-8134
Laser printers / imagesetters

Studio Management

Acius, Inc.
10351 Bubb Road
Cupertino, CA 95014
(408) 252-4444
4th Dimension

Adobe Systems Inc.
1585 Charleston Road
Mountain View, CA 94039
(415) 961-4400
TrueForms

Affinity Microsystems, Ltd.
1050 Walnut Street
Boulder, CO 80302
(800) 367-6771
Time Billing &
Client Receivables

Vendors

Studio management

Ashton-Tate
20101 Hamilton Avenue
Torrance, CA 90502
(213) 329-8000
Dbase Mac-database
Full Impact-spreadsheet

Blyth Software, Inc.
1065 E. Hillsdale Boulevard
Foster City, CA 94404
(415) 571-0222
Omnis 5-database

Brain Power Inc.
30497 Canwood Street
Agoura Hills, CA 91301
(800) 345-0519
Graphidex-graphic index

Chang Laboratories, Inc.
5300 Stevens Creek Blvd.
San Jose, CA 95129
(800) 972-8800
C.A.T.-
Contacts-Activities-Time

Claris Corporation
5201 Patrick Henry Drive
Santa Clara, CA 95052
(800) 334-3535
FileMaker II
SmartForm Designer
SmartForm Assistant

DeltaPoint, Inc.
200 Heritage Harbor
Monterey, CA 93940
(408) 648-4000
Trapeze-integrated
presentation

Exceiver Corporation
P.O. Box 671
Hopkins, MN 55343
(612) 938-3361
Time Billing

Fox Software, Inc.
134 W. South Boundary
Perrysburg, OH 43551
(419) 874-0162
FoxBase+/Mac

Highgate Cross & Cathey
130 West Liberty
Wheaton, IL 60187
(312) 653-2700
DesignSoft-time & billing

System Informix Software
16011 College Boulevard
Lenexa, KS 66219
(913) 492-3800
Wingz-Spreadsheet

Layered, Inc.
529 Main Street
Boston, MA 02129
(617) 242-7700
Insight-time & billing

Marvelin Corp.
3420 Ocean Park Blvd.
Santa Monica, CA 90405
(213) 450-6813
Business Filevision
Filevision IV

Microsoft Corp.
16011 N.E. 36th Way
Redmond, WA 98073
(800) 426-9400
Microsoft File
Excel-spreadsheet

Odesta Corp.
4084 Commercial Avenue
Northbrook, IL 60062
(312) 498-5615
Double Helix II

Power Up Software Corp.
2929 Campus Drive
San Mateo, CA 94403
(800) 851-2917
Fast Forms

Preferred Publishers, Inc.
5100 Poplar Avenue
Memphis, TN 38137
(901) 683-3383
DAtabase-desk accessory

Provue Development Corp.
15180 Transistor Lane
Huntington Beach, CA 92649
(714) 892-8199
Panorama

Satori Software
2815 Second Avenue
Seattle, WA 98121
(206) 443-0765
Project Billing

Shana Corporation
9650 20th Avenue
Edmonton Alberta Canada
(403) 463-3330
InFormed Software

Discoveries, Inc.
137 Krawski Drive
South Windsor, CT 06074
(203) 872-1024
RecordHolder Plus

Symmetry Corp.
761 E. University Drive
Mesa, AZ 85203
(800) 624-2485
PictureBase

Timeslips Software Corp.
239 Western Avenue
Essex, MA 01929
(800) 338-5314
Timeslips-time & billing

Multimedia

Aldus Corporation
411 First Avenue S.
Seattle, WA 98104
(206) 622-5500
Aldus Persuasion

Computer Associates
601 Gateway Blvd. S.
San Francisco, CA 94080
(415) 875-1600
CA-Cricket Presents

General Parametrics Corp.
1250 9th Street
Berkeley, CA 94710
(415) 524-3950
VideoShow

Letraset USA
40 Eisenhower Drive
Paramus, NJ 07653
(800) 526-9073
StandOut!-presentations

MacroMind, Inc.
410 Townsend
San Francisco, CA 94107
(415) 442-0200
VideoWorks II
MacroMind Director

Microsoft Corp.
16011 N.E. 36th Way
Redmond, WA 98073
(800) 426-9400
PowerPoint-presentations

Owl International Inc.
2800 156th Avenue SE
Bellevue, WA 98007
(206) 747-3203
Guide-Hypertext
software system

Silicon Beach Software
9770 Carroll Center Road
San Diego, CA 92126
(619) 695-6956
SuperCard-color
Hypermedia

Symantec Corporation
10201 Torre Avenue
Cupertino, CA 95104
(800) 441-7234
More II-
planning, writing
& desktop presentations

Communications

Hayes Microcomputer
P.O. Box 105203
Atlanta, GA 30348
(404) 441-1617
Communications

Farrallon Computing
2201 Dwight Way
Berkeley, CA 94704
(415) 849-2331
PhoneNet

Novell
122 East 1700 South
Provo, UT 84606
(800) 526-5463
Communications

Index

Index